the Vibrant Vegetarian

Vikki Leng

D1551103

HarperCollins*Publishers*

HarperCollins*Publishers*

First published in Australia in 1997
Reprinted in 1997
by HarperCollins*Publishers* Pty Limited
ACN 009 913 517
A member of the HarperCollins*Publishers* (Australia) Pty Limited Group
http://www.harpercollins.com.au

HarperCollins*Publishers*
25 Ryde Road, Pymble, Sydney, NSW 2073, Australia
31 View Road, Glenfield, Auckland 10, New Zealand
77-85 Fulham Palace Road, London W6 8JB, United Kingdom
Hazelton Lanes, 55 Avenue Road, Suite 2900, Toronto, Ontario M5R 3L2
and 1995 Markham Road, Scarborough, Ontario M1B 5M8, Canada
10 East 53rd Street, New York NY 10032, USA

National Library of Australia Cataloguing-in-Publication data:

Leng, Vikki, 1951–
The vibrant vegetarian.
Includes index.
ISBN 0 7322 5831 6.
1. Vegetarian cookery. I. Title.
641.5636

Photographic concept and styling by Joe Filshie and Georgina Dolling
Printed in Hong Kong By Skiva Printing and Binding Co., Ltd on 115gsm Matt Art

9 8 7 6 5 4 3 2   97 98 99

Contents

About the Author

From the age of eleven, when she started creating recipes for her family, Vikki Leng has always loved food and cooking. Her gregariousness and a flair for arousing enthusiasm in others led her to a career as an author, cooking demonstrator, food and nutrition consultant and media personality. With three children of her own (not to mention three cats and two dogs) she was a natural talent on children's television, where she showed countless thousands of children how much fun it could be to 'eat up your greens'.

An accomplished writer, Vikki has published twelve recipe books and manuals on how to prepare lighter, healthier meals, six of which are about her specialist area – vegetarian cooking. A qualified home economist, Vikki's inspiration for her innovative and stylish recipe ideas come from travelling and talking to fellow food lovers. She is actively involved with nutrition education and promotion activities for a variety of audiences, including employee groups at their own workplaces where her audiences enjoy her practical and entertaining presentations and her 'real food' approach. 'After all', says Vikki, 'People eat food, not nutrients.'

Vikki's most successful book, *A Vegetarian Feast*, was published by Angus & Robertson (an imprint of HarperCollins *Publishers*) in 1994.

Introduction

Food is here to be enjoyed, and those of us lucky enough to have ready access to a wonderful array of quality ingredients indeed have much to celebrate. Passionate cooks enjoy whipping up spur-of-the-moment creations and concocting wonderful dishes for friends and family. They know that good food need not be fussed over, and that it doesn't necessarily take hours to prepare. But it seems that many of us who lead busy lives believe we have less and less time to enjoy this convivial pastime. Many people I talk to say, 'I would enjoy cooking more if I only had the time.' To me, this is a real shame. I've been through busy periods in my life without resorting to wall-to-wall fast food, so I know it can be done!

As well as sharing some of my favourite recipes with you, I hope this book inspires you to enjoy the shopping, preparation and cooking of food. For shopping, cooking and eating are activities that we spend much of our life doing. However, this book does not merely focus on my survival tactics. More importantly, I hope it provides some valuable tips for enjoying all the processes involved in food preparation.

I get a kick out of becoming familiar with many of the properties of ingredients, including their sensory, aesthetic, physical, chemical and nutritional qualities. The next step for me is thinking up ideas of how to create enticing dishes from them. That's why my latest recipes for quick and easy dishes have been arranged according to their main ingredient. This is also helpful if you have a specific ingredient in the pantry and are at a loss as to what to do with it. Or you might crave a particular food, like feta, but can't think of a recipe for it.

Whatever the scenario, you'll find many time-saving ways to prepare a range of delicious common and not so common recipes in this book. And, rest assured, most of these ingredients do not require trips to specialty shops. The majority can be obtained from the larger supermarkets, fruit and vegetable markets and shops, others can be purchased from delicatessens, and some of my favourites are found in Asian grocery stores.

Vegetables and fruits would have to be my favourite foods. They are not only seducers of the senses but they are also a pleasure to prepare and wonderful to eat. Apart from the incredible colours, tastes, textures and fragrances that vegetables and fruits have to offer, they are a vital link in the foundation of good health. Recent research has demonstrated that vegetables play a key role in helping to protect our bodies against cancer and heart disease. And it seems the more fruit and vegetables we eat, the greater the protective element. So our growing interest in an international style of eating based on more vegetables and fruits, breads and cereals not only gives our senses a treat, but can help boost health and vitality as well.

When it comes to taking care of our health, most of us are well aware that we need to cut down on fat. It's so easy to get carried away with dolloping, scattering, spooning, splashing and pouring rich sauces, dressings and fatty ingredients on to our food. What better way to start a healthier way of eating than to discover that fruit, vegetables, bread and cereal-based snacks and meals can be equally delicious and satisfying? Throughout this book I provide notes on reducing fat in recipes. And don't forget, if you eat sensibly you'll still be able to enjoy the occasional crispy deep-fried morsel without feeling guilty and worrying about your health. It all comes back to remembering that life is to be enjoyed — not endured or mapped out, weighed and measured! You'll feel wonderful and — as an added bonus — you'll have more energy to celebrate life with.

Cook's Notes

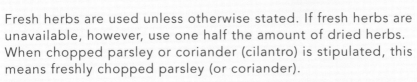

Fresh herbs are used unless otherwise stated. If fresh herbs are unavailable, however, use one half the amount of dried herbs. When chopped parsley or coriander (cilantro) is stipulated, this means freshly chopped parsley (or coriander).

When ginger is stipulated, use freshly grated root ginger. When garlic cloves are mentioned, use plump cloves for more flavour. Use freshly ground black pepper unless cracked black pepper is specified. There is a wide variety of chillies (chilli peppers) from mildly hot to excruciatingly fierce! Choose the type that suits your palate and that of your guests. To keep the heat moderate, seed the chillies before chopping or slicing them because much of their heat comes from the seeds. I usually use red chillies and vary the amount used in each recipe according to the heat of the chillies. All references in recipes are to fresh chillies; if you have dried chillies, use about half the given amount.

Use medium-sized fruits and vegetables unless a specific size is called for. Leave the skins on tomatoes unless peeled tomatoes are noted. Cup measurements are included as an additional guide.

When oil is called for, use a mild-flavoured oil such as canola; oils required for their distinctive flavours such as extra virgin olive oil, peanut oil and sesame oil are individually specified.

Use reduced-fat or low-fat dairy products when milk, yoghurt, cream cheese or sour cream are listed unless other varieties are called for. When cream is specified, use varieties that have been thickened with vegetable gum rather than gelatine (which is an animal product). Soy drink is interchangeable with cow's milk for all recipes.

Use reduced-salt soy sauce. When tofu is called for, soft or firm tofu is interchangeable, unless either is specified.

When flour is called for, use plain (all-purpose) flour.

When prepared baking trays (sheets) and cake tins (pans) are called for, simply use a pastry brush to brush them with a little oil or melted butter.

White A1 sugar, caster (superfine) and raw sugar are interchangeable unless a specific type is called for.

The microwave cooking times have been calculated according to the use of a 650-watt microwave oven. If your microwave oven is a lower wattage you will need to add 5 seconds per minute per 50 watts to the specified cooking times. If you have a higher wattage oven, subtract 5 seconds per minute per 50 watts from the specified cooking times. Remember to use only microwave-proof dishes and microwave-safe plastic wraps.

Apart from these notes, remember the most important point — to enjoy the art of cooking and allow your own creativity to flourish. Have fun!

Weights and Measures

For accurate measurements, you will need:

- a nest of four graduated measuring cups for measuring dry ingredients. These come in ¼, ½, ⅓ and 1-cup sizes;

- a standard measuring cup for measuring liquids;

- a 1-litre or 4-cup measuring jug for measuring large quantities of liquid. These jugs usually show both cup and metric measures and are marked in cups and millilitres, others in imperial fluid ounces;

- a set of graduated measuring spoons. The set includes a tablespoon, teaspoon, ½-teaspoon and ¼-teaspoon. Level spoon measures are used unless stipulated otherwise;

- scales. Usually marked nowadays in both metric and imperial measurements. Scales are needed for weighing vegetables and other bulky items.

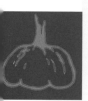

Weights and measures translations in this book are not exact equivalents, but are brought to the nearest round figure; however, they still preserve the correct balance of ingredients. To retain that balance, follow either metric or imperial, never a mixture.

Spoon and Cup Measurements

	Australia	New Zealand	United Kingdom	United States
1 tablespoon	20 mL	15 mL	½ fl oz (14 mL)	½ fl oz (14 mL)
1 cup	250 mL	250 mL	8 fl oz (237 mL)	8 fl oz (237 mL)

All countries use the same teaspoon measurements.

Preheat the oven

Always preheat an oven, unless you are reheating food. The time this takes varies with the oven. The usual time to reach a required oven temperature ranges from 15 to 20 minutes. Check the instruction book for your oven.

The correct oven temperature is essential to the success of a dish. It makes pastry crisp, and a soufflé or cake rise. Sometimes oven temperatures are changed during cooking, e.g. high heat for a crispy topping, then low to cook the filling.

Oven Temperatures and Gas Marks

Celsius	Fahrenheit	Gas Marks	Heat
110°C	225°F	¼ (S)	very cool
120°C	250°F	½ (S)	very cool
140°C	275°F	1	cool
150°C	300°F	2	cool
160°C	325°F	3	moderate
180°C	350°F	4	moderate
190°C	375°F	5	fairly hot
200°C	400°F	6	fairly hot
220°C	425°F	7	hot
230°C	450°F	8	very hot
240°C	475°F	9	very hot
260°C	500°F	10	very hot

Note: gas mark S is a special setting on some ovens, used for cooking slowly, e.g. for meringues.

Planning & Preparation

Clever planning is a real sanity saver for it can make the difference between panic and an enjoyable cooking experience. If you're a busy person, the more organised your kitchen is for the onslaught of hordes demanding quick snacks and impromptu meals the better. Here are a few tips I have found useful.

Time Planning

Use time wisely. This includes allowing yourself enough space for rest and relaxation. So it is important to carefully consider the amount of time you have available for shopping, preparation, cooking and eating. Cooking up a feast of dishes when you are rushed is missing the point. It would be better to settle for preparing a stunning sandwich and a lovely fresh fruit platter than to try to concoct an impressive spread that either goes wrong or leaves you feeling exhausted. This way, you are able to enjoy yourself and the company of those you cook for. Postpone busy cooking sprees for a time when you can potter around the kitchen and enjoy it, for example at weekends and during holiday breaks.

Shopping

Keep a list of items you need which you can add to as you run out of them. I find it is handy to have a wad of paper (usually recycled from my office) and a pen in a prominent place in the kitchen. And have patience. Building up a well-stocked pantry of basic ingredients takes time. A good piece of advice is, don't go shopping when you are hungry, for you will inevitably return with far more food than you bargained for! Watch out for convenient forms of ingredients that you use frequently, such as canned tomatoes, so you can have a ready supply on hand.

Shopping Checklists

When planning the most effective way of shopping for fresh produce, become aware of the seasonal availability of fresh fruits, vegetables and herbs. In season, these key ingredients are likely to be more flavoursome, at their peak of freshness and more economical.

Checklist for supermarket and delicatessen shopping

■ canned (tinned) goods: tomatoes, tomato paste (purée), beans, fruit in its own juice, coconut cream and coconut milk;

■ bottled goods: pasta sauce, pesto, curry paste, oils and vinegars;

■ marinated foods: olives, artichoke hearts, sun-dried tomatoes, capsicums (sweet peppers), 'bread and butter' cucumbers, gherkins, pickled onions and capers;

■ dry goods: rice, pasta, noodles, couscous, dried beans, peas and lentils, nuts, seeds, dried fruits, flour, active dried yeast, sugar, dried herbs and spices and breakfast cereals;

■ condiments: soy sauce, Tobasco Sauce and grainy mustard;

■ chilled dairy foods: milk, butter, cheese, yoghurt, buttermilk, sour cream, cream and ice cream.

Checklist for Asian grocery store shopping

■ bottled or vacuum-packed vegetables: e.g. pickled daikon radish (page 49) and pickled ginger;

■ dry goods: rice, noodles, poppadums, beans, peas, lentils, nuts and seeds;

■ chilled foods: tofu, tempeh and wonton skins;

■ fresh produce: Chinese greens, root ginger, chillies (chilli peppers), garlic, chives, coriander (cilantro) and spring onions (scallions).

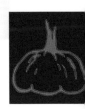

Equipment

You don't need to have the kitchen of a five-star hotel to enjoy cooking, but having some basic equipment will certainly help get you started.

Small but essential

- pastry brush to keep the use of oil to a minimum; useful for brushing the top of bread with water or milk and for brushing tomato paste (purée) over pizza bases;
- a good solid garlic crusher (press);
- ginger grater (the bamboo type that can be picked up for a song in an Asian grocery store is my favourite);
- kitchen scissors for snipping fresh herbs and cutting mountain (lavash or sorj) bread;
- piping bag for piping Lemon Cream Cheese on to pancakes and stuffing fruit;
- vegetable peeler for peeling hard vegetables like pumpkin and potato, fresh root ginger and for shaving hard cheeses;
- wooden spoons;
- rubber or plastic pan scrapers;
- egg lifters or thick spatulas;
- serving spoons.

Knives

You can get by with one or two knives. Choose the ones that feel right for you, according to a suitable weight, comfortable handle and durability. A good basic set consists of a large cook's knife, one or two smaller knives (for example, a paring knife and a serrated stainless-steel knife) and a chopper — great for cutting solid vegetables like pumpkin.

Pots and pans

- large soup pot for hearty soups, stews and hot pots and because it's a good idea to make dishes which need slow cooking in large quantities so that you can stash them away in the refrigerator and freezer for use when you are really busy;
- colander, strainer and sieve;
- small and medium-sized saucepans for cooking smaller amounts of food and steaming vegetables in a steamer insert;
- small and large frying pans (skillets) and a wok (all with lids, if possible) for cooking quick dishes such as braised vegetables and stir-fries.

Food processor and/or blender

This is a sizeable investment, so choose the best processor your budget will comfortably allow. Consider the size of the bowl, which should be able to process food in the amounts you regularly use.

Microwave oven

A microwave is useful for cooking vegetables without fat, for whipping up custards and thickened sauces without having them stick to a pan and for softening or melting butter or chocolate without overheating them. It is also a whiz for efficient use of energy because you don't have to preheat a whole oven. Another advantage is that using a microwave keeps both you and your kitchen cool in summer because it only heats the food, not the whole oven or its surroundings.

One drawback of using a microwave is that it can be a little fiddly — you often have to stop-start the cooking and take the food out periodically to stir or rearrange it. I don't often use a microwave for cooking whole dishes, but it is useful for part-cooking certain ingredients.

Plates and platters

I recommend purchasing several colourful plates or platters, whether they be inexpensive or second-hand, or good solid ones that you can keep for ever. These are great for informal meals when you want to set the food out in the middle of the table for all to select as you chat and pass dishes. Great for both indoor meals at any time of the year and for outdoor eating in the warmer months.

Pre-preparation

This is an especially important step if you really want to take full advantage of the wonderful variety of dried legumes that are available and regularly incorporate them in tasty dishes. I have made it a habit to soak a week's supply of dried beans, peas and lentils as soon as I unpack them from after shopping. Even if you realise later that you won't have time to cook them, you can still drain and store them in a container in the freezer for later use. The same applies to beans, peas and lentils after they have been cooked. Make the time to cook up generous batches of your favourite legumes (page 128) so that they can be included in future dishes, no matter how short of time you are when the actual meal preparation time is upon you.

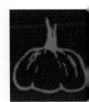

If you feel inspired to cook as I often do, play a CD or tape of your favourite music and really enjoy this time. Have storage containers and labels on hand so you can complete the entire task of cooking and packing the food away in one fell swoop. Believe me, you will be so grateful for those little tubs of prepared treats when you're tired and longing for a comforting solo meal or when unexpected guests arrive and you wish to extend your hospitality to a quick and tasty meal without creating havoc in the kitchen.

Here are some ingredients and dishes that are perfect for pre-preparing and storing in the refrigerator or freezer for later use:

- Quick and Tasty Pasta Sauce (page 91)
- Roasted Eggplant Rounds (page 21)
- Roasted Capsicum (page 16)
- Quick Tomato Chutney (page 24)
- Golden Pumpkin Soup (page 28)
- Quick Pickled Carrots (page 32)
- Crimson Carrots (page 33)
- Fruity Blissballs (page 60)
- Pesto Sauce (page 92)
- Cooked Brown Rice (page 102)
- Basic Polenta (page 114)
- Basic Cooked Legumes (page 128)
- All-time-favourite Lentil Burgers (page 137)
- Red Lentil and Vegetable Burgers (page 139).

Cooking

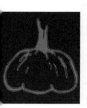

Long gone are the days when many of us routinely sat down together to a two or three-course meal in the evenings. It seems meals have become more impromptu, casual affairs. This does not mean that the quality of the food we serve should be compromised, or that we can no longer enjoy meals. We simply need to be realistic about the type of food we can prepare, given the limited time we have to spend in the kitchen. When preparing meals, choose a range of dishes that can be cooked at the same time without fuss — cook baked vegetables together and roast nuts and seeds in the same oven as you are cooking a pizza or a fruit crumble. This is not just a clever use of time, but optimises your use of basic commodities like gas and electricity.

Presenting and Garnishing Dishes

Even the simplest of meals can be special. Sometimes all it takes is arranging the food attractively on a colourful plate and making use of a simple garnish. These are a few of my favourite garnishes:

■ tiny yellow and red teardrop tomatoes ■ cherry tomatoes ■ lemon or lime wedges ■ diced red onion ■ freshly chopped parsley ■ finely diced capsicums (sweet peppers) of varying colours ■ dustings of cracked black pepper or sweet paprika and strips of toasted nori (page 104) ■ whole berries ■ clusters or pairs of cherries ■ edible blossoms (such as pansies, nasturtiums, borage, marigolds, violets, carnations, geraniums, jasmine and sweet pea) ■ roasted nuts and seeds and thick (Greek-style) yoghurt.

Enjoying Food

This is the most important point of all, for no matter how long you spend in the kitchen performing wonderful tricks with the ingredients, much of the effect will be lost if you, the cook, don't get to actually enjoy the food. So, whether you are eating alone or with friends, indoors or outdoors, at breakfast or dinner, make a point of taking time to savour the flavours of the food. Even when dining alone on a quick meal of grilled cheese on toast, treat yourself to a special variation — spread a little pesto sauce on your toast before melting the cheese on top, then top it all off with a generous spoonful of salsa or salad such as Crunchy Red Cabbage Salad (page 46) and a smattering of halved or sliced cherry tomatoes.

Likewise, enjoy the times when friends drop in by serving the food on platters in the middle of the table. This is a good recipe for getting the conversation rolling and enjoying the visual impact of the food.

Vibrant

Vegetab

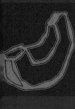

les

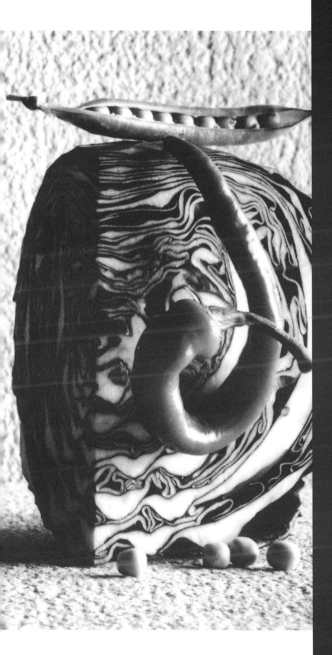

What glorious foods vegetables and fruits are! I can't imagine more inspiring ingredients to cook with. Even if you feel a little 'ho hum' about the time you need to spend in the kitchen, there's something about vegetables and fruits that makes it all worthwhile and, dare I venture, enjoyable!

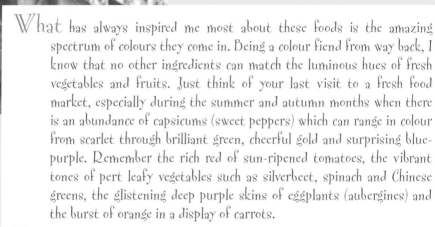

What has always inspired me most about these foods is the amazing spectrum of colours they come in. Being a colour fiend from way back, I know that no other ingredients can match the luminous hues of fresh vegetables and fruits. Just think of your last visit to a fresh food market, especially during the summer and autumn months when there is an abundance of capsicums (sweet peppers) which can range in colour from scarlet through brilliant green, cheerful gold and surprising blue-purple. Remember the rich red of sun-ripened tomatoes, the vibrant tones of pert leafy vegetables such as silverbeet, spinach and Chinese greens, the glistening deep purple skins of eggplants (aubergines) and the burst of orange in a display of carrots.

Fruits can be equally spectacular. You can be mesmerised by rich red sun-ripened berries even before you catch sight of them. This is because another of their seductive qualities comes in to play — fragrance. Remember the alluring scent of the ripe mangoes you bought, even though you hadn't thought you needed them when you set out for the market? Or the quinces you hadn't seen since your childhood. Alerted to their existence by a familiar sweet, yet distinctive perfume, you bought just a few because you couldn't resist their cheerful bright yellow hue. Even if you don't have access to fresh food markets, many local fruit and vegetable shops display their wares in an equally inviting way, especially those which have an inbuilt passion for these wonderful foods and a cheerful commitment to great service.

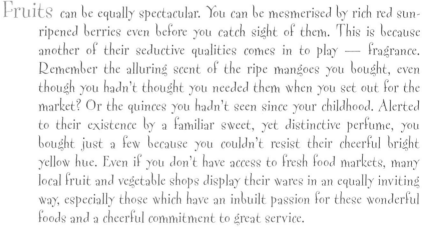

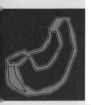

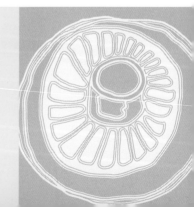

Many supermarkets also carry a range of quality fresh produce, and I'm convinced this is where customers who have never met before dare to exchange small talk as they reach for the best pears or weigh their grapes. (I'm sure that when the ice has been thus broken, advice is offered and taken on such important matters as how to cook zucchini (courgettes) or whether to leave the skins on sweet potatoes before you bake them.) Even if you can't buy fresh produce, never fear, for even frozen, canned (tinned) and bottled vegetables can add a splash of colour and a burst of flavour to your next snack or meal.

Having sung the praises of the magnificent colours of vegetables, the next quality that fascinates me is their amazing range of flavours, especially those of the new varieties available to us. Nowadays there are also many new ways of preparing common vegetables that we can learn from people from diverse cultures.

Although most people know that vegetables are good for their health, many think that such food is boring. This is often because they have only eaten vegetables that have had the life, taste and texture boiled out of them! I'm sure many of us at one time or another have had to endure soggy, overcooked 'army green' cabbage or broccoli or flavourless, boiled, mashed and probably (I shudder to think) lumpy pumpkin.

Thank goodness those days are gone and we can now enjoy colourful Asian-inspired vegetable stir-fries laced with the flavours of sesame, garlic and ginger or the robust flavours of garlicky Mediterranean dishes concocted from eggplants (aubergines), capsicums (sweet peppers) and tomatoes. Vegetables have never been such an exciting food to prepare.

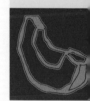

Roasted

capsicum (sweet pepper) makes a delicious addition to antipasto platters, main dishes, sandwiches, salads, dips and sauces. Any colour of capsicum can be roasted, of course, but my favourite is the sweet red variety because this process intensifies both the colour and the sweetness.

Ingredients

2 capsicums (sweet peppers), cut into 4 lengthways, seeds removed

Serves 4

Method

Roast the capsicum under a hot grill (broiler) until the skin becomes blistered and charred.

Immediately place the capsicum in a brown paper bag or a plastic bag and set it aside until it is cool enough to handle, about 10 minutes. This keeps the steam from the hot capsicum in the bag so that the flesh softens and the skin can be easily peeled off.

If not using straightaway, place the bag in the refrigerator and continue with the preparation up to 3 or 4 days later.

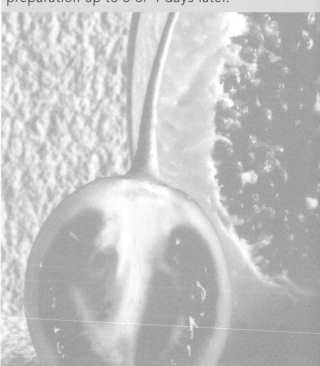

Hooray for colour, especially the richness of scarlet. But even though the hue seems to be the main attraction of this sauce, it is really the wonderful flavour that wins many a heart and taste bud. It must be the winning combination of the sweetness of roasted capsicum (sweet pepper) and the 'oomph' of fresh garlic. Try serving a pool of this luscious sauce around Grilled Polenta (page 115) or Quick Polenta Shapes (page 115), drizzle it over Baked Jacket Potatoes (page 59) or serve with Golden Potato Wedges (page 40).

Method

Using a blender or food processor, purée the capsicum flesh with the vegetable stock, vinegar and garlic until it reaches the desired consistency. I like to make this sauce velvety smooth while others prefer a slightly chunky texture.

Season to taste with the pepper and serve.

If not needed straightaway, store in a glass jar in the refrigerator for 2–3 days — an ideal way to store this sauce because just one look at its incredible colour is sure to inspire you to use it to liven up your next quick snack or meal.

Ingredients

2 red capsicums (sweet peppers), roasted and peeled

½ cup (125 mL/4 fl oz) vegetable stock (see below)

2 teaspoons balsamic vinegar

1–2 garlic cloves, crushed (pressed)

pepper

Makes about 1½ cups (375 mL/12 fl oz)

Vegetable Stock

If you are likely to have a stock pot on the stove for boiling up your own stock, this is ideal, for in this way you can use up most of your vegetable scraps. Store washed vegetable skins and trimmings such as the tops of spring onions (scallions), ends of carrot, washed onion skins and the coarse base part of celery in a plastic bag in the refrigerator and add other bits and pieces over a period of 3 or 4 days. Avoid using cabbage, Brussels sprouts, broccoli or cauliflower for the flavour of these vegetables is too overpowering, and can also develop a pungent edge with prolonged cooking.

When you have the chance, pop them all into a large saucepan, cover them with water and bring them to the boil. Boil the concoction for 1 hour while you get on with other things. If you don't have time to cook up a pot of stock, then the scraps can go into the compost — no love lost!

If you don't have the time or inclination to make your own vegetable stock this way, simply use miso (page 161) or good-quality stock cubes which aren't laden with salt. Miso keeps well in the refrigerator so it's easy to have a steady supply on hand.

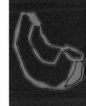

A good garnish for soups and hot pots that need a burst of both colour and flavour, I love serving this salsa over All-in-one Soup (page 36) with a sizzling frying pan (skillet) of cornbread (page 117) to calm down the heat from the chilli.

Method

Ingredients

1 red capsicum (sweet pepper), seeded and diced finely, about 1½ cups (300 g/ 10 oz)

1 green capsicum (sweet pepper), seeded and diced finely, about 1½ cups (300 g/ 10 oz)

2 garlic cloves, crushed (pressed)

1 chilli (chilli pepper), seeded and sliced finely

3–4 spring onions (scallions), sliced, green tops included

¼ teaspoon cracked black pepper

pinch of salt

2 teaspoons balsamic vinegar

juice of ½ lemon or lime, about 2 tablespoons

Makes about 3 cups (750 mL/24 fl oz)

Combine all the ingredients well.

Serve at once, or, if not using straightaway, store the salsa in a screw-top jar in the refrigerator for up to 1 week.

A Swirl or a Squiggle?

Scarlet Sauce is delightful to have on hand to swirl over piping hot Golden Pumpkin Soup (page 28) or Creamy Parsnip Soup (page 35). And what more perfect sauce could you ask for when you're adding a squiggle of colour in true Crescent Dragonwagon fashion (page 37)?

The colour in paper streamers inspired its name, though this dish is as tasty as it is colourful. A great topping for Baked Jacket Potatoes (page 39), polenta and all manner of hot pasta dishes and salads.

Method

Heat the oil in a medium-sized saucepan, add the capsicum and zucchini and stir over a medium to high heat for 2 minutes.

Stir in the spring onions, cabbage and lemon juice, then cover and cook over a medium heat for 10 minutes.

Drizzle with the honey and season to taste with the pepper.

Can be served hot, warm or cold.

Ingredients

2 teaspoons oil

2 red capsicums (sweet peppers), seeded and cut into thin strips, about 3 cups (600 g/ 1¼ lb)

1 zucchini (courgette), trimmed and cut into thin sticks, about 1 cup

6 spring onions (scallions) cut into 4–5 cm (1½–2 in) lengths, then into strips, green tops included

1 cup (90 g/3 oz) thin strips of red cabbage

juice of ½ lemon, about 2 tablespoons

1 teaspoon honey

pepper

Serves 4

Sweating or Sauteing?

Sweating and sauteing involve stirring or tossing food over a fairly high heat in some kind of fat. This both develops the flavour of food and cooks and softens it quickly.

The difference between the two methods is that sweating involves cooking with the lid on the pan so that the vegetables cook mostly in their own juices, thus minimising the amount of oil required to prevent the vegetables sticking to the pan. Sauteing is usually done in a considerable amount of fat, with the lid off the pan.

I prefer the sauteing method, especially when I am in a hurry because it ensures thorough cooking quickly without the flavour loss associated with boiling. That's also why I like starting the cooking of most of my soups, vegetable braises and sauces this way.

Streamers

19

Braised Capsicum

This is a colourful, flavoursome side dish that has a surprisingly tender texture. It is delicious served simply with fresh crusty bread or used to dress up polenta or pasta dishes. It also makes a colourful topping for Baked Jacket Potatoes (page 39) along with light sour cream and a liberal dusting of cracked black pepper. For the most dramatic effect, use capsicums (sweet peppers) of varying colours.

Ingredients

2–3 teaspoons olive oil

2 medium-sized red (Spanish) onions, cut into thin half rings, about 2 cups (300 g/ 10 oz)

3 capsicums (sweet peppers), seeded and cut into thick strips, about 4 cups (800 g/1¾ lb)

2 garlic cloves, crushed (pressed)

**1 large firm but ripe tomato, diced, or
1 cup (250 g/8 fl oz) canned (tinned) crushed tomatoes**

2 teaspoons balsamic vinegar (optional)

cracked black pepper

Serves 4

Method

Heat the oil in a large frying pan (skillet) or saucepan with a lid, then add the onion and capsicum. Stir over a medium heat for 1–2 minutes, then cook with the lid on the pan for 15 minutes, stirring occasionally.

Add the garlic and tomato and cook, covered, for a further 5 minutes. Season to taste with the vinegar (if using) and the pepper.

Delicious served hot or at room temperature.

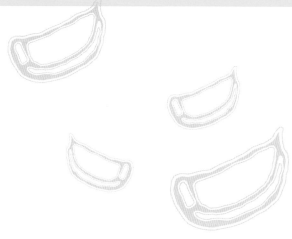

These are simple and quick to make and can be roasting in the oven while you get on with other things. Serve them as part of an antipasto platter, or as a delicious sandwich filling with crispy salad greens and fresh tomato slices. They are also handy to tuck away in storage containers in the refrigerator to be used later on top of pizzas or in vegetable braises such as ratatouille. However, according to my taste testers, the most luscious way to use them is in Roasted Eggplant Sandwiches (page 25).

Method

Preheat the oven to 200°C/400°F.

Using a pastry brush, brush a baking tray (sheet) with a little of the oil. Combine the remaining oil with the garlic in a small bowl or jar.

Arrange the eggplant slices on the baking tray. Brush the tops of the eggplant slices with the garlic and oil mixture.

Bake for 15 minutes.

Ingredients

1 tablespoon olive oil

2–3 garlic cloves, crushed (pressed)

2 good-sized eggplants (aubergines), each cut into 12 slices crossways

Serves 4–6

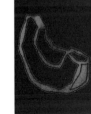

Low-fat Tip for Cooking Eggplant (Aubergine)

Roasting eggplants is the perfect low-fat way to prepare this vegetable because it has an insatiable appetite for oil. If you fry eggplant the oil is soaked up as soon as it is added to the pan. On the other hand, when you roast it at least you can control the amount of oil you add.

Once you have roasted eggplant on hand, this dip can literally be assembled in minutes.

Ingredients

1 quantity Roasted
Eggplant Rounds
(page 21)

1–2 garlic cloves,
crushed (pressed)

juice of 1 lemon,
about
4 tablespoons

2 tablespoons
tahini

1 tablespoon
soy sauce

few drops
Tabasco Sauce

pepper

Makes about
1½ cups
(375 mL/12 fl oz)

Method

Place the eggplant, garlic, lemon juice, tahini and soy sauce in a food processor and blend until smooth.

Season to taste with the Tabasco Sauce and the pepper.

Garlic for a Flavour Burst

Although I understand that not everyone is as enamoured of garlic as me, when I stipulate a clove of garlic in a recipe, I mean a really voluptuous one. Why bother with a token sliver just to tick it off as you go through the ingredients for your recipe? However, there is an exception to the rule. Go gently with the garlic when you want the overall flavour of the dish you are preparing to be less dramatic, or if you wish to enhance the delicate flavours of food such as zucchini. And remember, slicing and chopping garlic impart a more subtle flavour than crushing it.

These 'sandwiches' are for those who like robust flavours, for all the ingredients in this dish are strongly flavoured, except for the mozzarella cheese, which provides an interesting contrast in taste and its characteristically stretchy texture. The recipe uses small slices of roasted eggplant as the 'bread' part of the sandwich, with pesto and mozzarella as the filling.

You can serve Eggplant Sandwiches uncooked as an appetiser or finger food. If baked and eaten hot or warm, I like to serve them with Grilled Polenta (page 115) and Scarlet Sauce (page 17). Or, if you are looking for a fresh accompaniment, serve with a simple salad of greens with a vinaigrette dressing.

Method

Preheat the oven to 180°C/350°F and prepare an ovenproof dish by brushing it with a little of the oil.

Cut the capsicum into 8 rough squares. Then cut the mozzarella into 16 slices.

Arrange 8 Roasted Eggplant Rounds in the ovenproof dish. Spread the eggplant slices with 2 tablespoons of the Pesto Sauce, then top with half the slices of mozzarella. Repeat with 8 more eggplant slices, the remaining Pesto Sauce and mozzarella and the remaining eggplant slices.

Arrange a good-sized piece of roasted capsicum on top of each 'sandwich', then brush with the remaining oil.

Dust with cracked black pepper and bake for 5–10 minutes only to prevent overcooking.

Ingredients

1 red capsicum (sweet pepper), roasted and peeled

250 g (8 oz) mozzarella cheese

24 Roasted Eggplant Rounds (page 21)

4 tablespoons Pesto Sauce (page 92)

½ teaspoon olive oil

cracked black pepper

Makes 8 sandwiches

A Non-dairy Version

Use drained firm tofu instead of mozzarella cheese for a change. This recipe suits the blandness of tofu which benefits from absorbing the strong flavours from the accompanying ingredients.

The natural sweetness of apples and currants in this recipe counteracts the acidity of the tomatoes as well as providing an interesting texture and colour contrast. This quick chutney is a welcome companion for burgers, filo (phyllo) pastry parcels, flans and sandwiches. It is excellent with Grilled Polenta (page 115) too and a good dollop or two can transform a simple snack of cheese on toast into a really scrumptious dish.

Method

Ingredients

2 teaspoons olive oil

2 onions, diced finely, about 2 cups (300 g/10 oz)

2 green apples, skin left on, diced finely

2–4 garlic cloves, crushed (pressed)

6 spring onions (scallions), sliced, green tops included

5 tomatoes, diced, about 5 cups (1.25 kg 250 g/2 lb)

2–3 tablespoons dried currants

pepper

Makes about 6 cups (1.5 litres/2½ imp pints)

Place the oil in a medium-sized saucepan and heat over a medium to high heat. Add the onion and stir for a minute or so. Cover and cook over a medium heat for 5 minutes.

Add the apple and garlic and stir once more. Cover and cook for 5 minutes, then stir in the spring onions, tomato and currants. Cook, covered, for 10 minutes, then season with the pepper.

If not using at once, store in a covered container in the refrigerator for up to 1 week.

Served hot or cold, this sauce adds both a burst of flavour and a splash of colour to a variety of dishes. It is especially good drizzled over your favourite nachos or burritos just before serving.

Method

Heat the oil and stir-fry the onion, garlic and chilli (or chilli powder) over a medium heat for 2 minutes.

Add the tomato and the apple juice and bring the mixture to the boil. Reduce the heat and simmer gently, covered, for 10 minutes.

Remove from the heat and stir in the honey.

Serve as it is or, using a food processor or blender, blend until smooth.

Ingredients

2 teaspoons oil

1 onion, finely chopped, about 1 cup (150 g/5 oz)

2–3 garlic cloves, crushed (pressed)

½–1 teaspoon finely chopped seeded chillies (chilli peppers) or ¼ teaspoon chilli powder

3 ripe tomatoes, peeled and chopped, about 3 cups (500 g/1 lb)

½ cup (125 mL/ 4 fl oz) apple juice

1 teaspoon honey

Makes about 4 cups (1 litre/1¾ imp pints)

Delicious and refreshing served atop piping hot nachos, tacos or burritos, or used as a stunning garnish on top of thick soups which have a dollop of light sour cream or yoghurt floating on top. As this is such a simple recipe, you can whip it up just when you need it, and it really is best when freshly prepared. However, it will keep for a day or two in the refrigerator. After that, if there is any left over, fling it into a soup, stew or pasta sauce rather than waste it.

Ingredients

1 small red (Spanish) onion, diced finely, about 1 cup (150 g/5 oz)

2 firm ripe tomatoes, diced, about 2 cups (375 g/12 oz) *or* 12 cherry tomatoes, halved

few drops Tabasco Sauce

2–3 tablespoons chopped coriander (cilantro) *or* sliced chives

cracked black pepper

Makes about 1 cup (250 mL/8 fl oz)

Method

Combine all the ingredients thoroughly in a mixing bowl.

If not serving at once, store in an airtight container in the refrigerator for 1 to 2 days only, to retain the fresh flavour.

A Carnival of Colour

When they are available, be sure to add some halved yellow teardrop tomatoes to this salsa.

This is a perfect recipe to entice those with jaded appetites — the creamy texture of avocado is offset beautifully by the sharpness of lemon or lime juice and the heat of the chillies. Avocado Hot Stuff is good for topping nachos, tacos and burritos and is a delicious filling for pita bread or mountain bread.

Method

Combine the lemon (or lime) juice with the garlic.

Place the avocado flesh in a medium-sized bowl and spoon the lemon mixture over. Toss carefully to ensure the avocado dice are coated with the juice as this will prevent the flesh from discolouring.

Scatter the chopped chillies, onion (or spring onions) and parsley (or coriander) over, then carefully mix them with the avocado, taking care not to break the flesh up too much.

Serve as soon as possible to retain the fresh flavour and colour.

Ingredients

juice of 1½ lemons or limes, about 6 tablespoons

2 garlic cloves, crushed (pressed)

1 medium to large avocado, pip removed, peeled and cut into large dice

½–1 teaspoon finely chopped seeded chillies (chilli peppers)

¼ red (Spanish) onion, diced finely, about ¼ cup (60 g/ 2 oz) or 4 spring onions (scallions), sliced finely, green tops included

¼ cup chopped parsley or coriander (cilantro)

Makes about 2 cups (500 mL/16 fl oz)

Sweet and nutty with a thick creamy texture, this soup marries well with moist black rye bread. For this particular soup I like to use soy drink in place of the milk for a change. This is a lovely soup for a light lunch or dinner followed by a fresh green salad and wedges of your favourite cheese.

Method

Ingredients

2 teaspoons oil

2 large onions, diced, about 2 cups (300 g/10 oz)

800 g (¼ lb) pumpkin, peeled and chopped, about 5 cups

2 garlic cloves, crushed (pressed)

4 cups (1 litre/ 1¾ imp pints) vegetable stock

2 cups (500 mL/ 16 fl oz) milk

pepper

3 tablespoons chopped coriander (cilantro) or parsley

Serves 4–6

Place the oil in a saucepan, add the onion and stir over a medium heat for 1 minute. Cover and cook for 5 minutes, stirring now and then.

Add the pumpkin and stir well, then cover and cook for 5 minutes more, stirring occasionally.

Add the garlic and stock and bring the mixture to the boil. Reduce the heat and simmer for 20 minutes, stirring occasionally to prevent the vegetables from sticking to the pan.

Using a food processor or blender, blend the soup with the milk until smooth.

Season to taste with pepper and reheat without boiling. Just before serving, sprinkle with coriander (or parsley).

Add a Splash of Colour for a Special Meal

Go no further than a swirl of Scarlet Sauce (page 17) or try Green Pea and Coriander Sauce (page 37). Either sauce looks stunning with that brilliant golden pumpkin hue as a backdrop.

Garlic is one of my favourite ingredients for providing a hearty flavour to food. Mushrooms seem to lap it up and develop a whole other dimension to their character. This recipe goes well as an accompaniment with pasta dishes, Grilled Polenta (page 115), or savoury tarts or flans.

Method

Heat the oil in a frying pan (skillet) and cook the spring onions and garlic over a low to medium heat to prevent the garlic from burning.

Add the mushrooms and shake the pan over the heat to ensure the mushrooms are evenly coated with the oil. Cook, uncovered, for 2 minutes, then cover and cook, stirring every now and then, for 5 minutes.

Add the flour and cook, stirring, for 1 minute. Add the soy sauce. Then add the stock (or water) and stir over a medium heat for 2–3 minutes.

Stir in the parsley and season to taste with the pepper.

Fresh Parsley

Gone are the days when parsley was used as a last-minute token garnish when you couldn't think of anything else to use. Now available year-round in temperate climates, fresh parsley, whether it be the beautiful Italian flat-leaf variety or the curly crisp-leaf sort, is a wonderful ingredient in its own right. Think of the amount of parsley it takes to make a tabouli salad. And there's a bonus to using generous amounts of parsley because it is rich in beta-carotene (vitamin A), vitamin C, and iron and calcium.

A handful of freshly chopped parsley will liven up a bubbling pot of minestrone or an aromatic pasta sauce. And a scattering of coarsely chopped parsley over freshly cooked pasta before it is tossed with even the simplest of sauces can add to its appeal.

Ingredients

1 tablespoon olive oil

6 spring onions (scallions), sliced, green tops included

4–5 garlic cloves, crushed (pressed)

500 g (1 lb) mushrooms trimmed and sliced, about 4 cups

2 tablespoons plain (all-purpose) flour

2 tablespoons soy sauce

½ cup (125 mL/ 4 fl oz) vegetable stock or water

¼ cup chopped parsley

pepper

Serves 4

I love using slightly peppery or bitter greens such as radish or beetroot (beet) tops. However, silverbeet, spinach or curly endive also go well in this dish, and are usually more readily available. Try serving it as a side dish, or tossed through freshly cooked noodles or pasta.

Method

Ingredients

2–3 teaspoons sesame oil

8 spring onions (scallions), sliced, green tops included

3 garlic cloves, crushed (pressed)

500 g (1 lb) mushrooms trimmed and sliced, about 4 cups

½ cup (125 mL/ 4 fl oz) vegetable stock

500 g (1 lb) chopped or shredded greens, about 4 cups

1 tablespoon soy sauce

1 teaspoon honey

pepper

Serves 4

Heat the oil in a wok or large frying pan (skillet) and add the spring onion. Stir over a medium heat for 1 minute.

Add the garlic and mushrooms and cover and cook for 5 minutes, stirring occasionally to prevent the mushrooms sticking to the pan.

Next, add the vegetable stock, cover and cook for 5 minutes more.

Add the greens, and cover and cook for 3 minutes, or until the greens have wilted down but are still a brilliant colour.

Drizzle the soy sauce and honey over and toss the vegetables to make sure they are all coated well.

Season to taste with the pepper.

Rich in colour and sweet and nutty in flavour, this soup will be popular with all members of the family. One extra my family and friends love is a sprinkling of roasted cashews on top of the soup, and a dusting of cracked black pepper adds the special lift that this soup needs. A little greenery doesn't go astray either, so I often scatter some snipped chives or finely sliced spring onion (scallion) tops over too.

Method

Place the oil in a saucepan, add the carrot and onion and stir over a medium heat for 1 minute. Place the lid on the pan and cook gently for 10 minutes.

Add the stock and bring the mixture to the boil, stirring occasionally. Reduce the heat and simmer for 15 minutes or until the carrots are tender.

Add the milk and blend until smooth using a food processor or blender.

Reheat without boiling and season to taste with the pepper.

Serve dusted with pepper.

Ingredients

2 teaspoons oil

1 kg (2 lb) carrots, scrubbed and diced, about 6 cups

2 large onions, diced, about 2 cups (300 g/10 oz)

3 cups (750 mL/ 24 fl oz) vegetable stock

2 cups (500 mL/ 16 fl oz) milk

pepper

Serves 4–6

Thick or Thin?

I love really thick soups which turn out almost like purées. But if you prefer a thinner consistency, add more stock or milk when blending the soup. You may then need to adjust the flavour by adding a little extra pepper or even a few drops of Tabasco Sauce.

These are fabulous served with Crimson Carrots (page 55) or, along with Red Cabbage Pickle (page 45), make an ideal crunchy and colourful filling for pita bread or mountain bread sandwiches or nori rolls.

Ingredients

2 cups (500 mL/ 16 fl oz) white vinegar

pinch of salt

2 tablespoons sugar

¼ teaspoon cracked black pepper

250 g (8 oz) diced carrots or thin carrot sticks, about 1 cup

Makes about 1 cup (250 g/8 oz)

Method

Place the vinegar, salt, sugar and pepper into a small saucepan and bring the mixture to the boil.

Add the carrots and boil for 2 minutes.

Remove from the heat and allow the mixture to stand for 5 minutes to allow further cooking and to give the flavours a chance to infuse.

Drain the juice from the carrots (retaining for later use — see opposite) and serve at once.

Or put both carrots and juice into a small jar and set aside to cool. They can be stored in the refrigerator for up to 1 week.

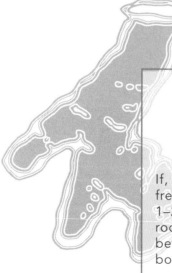

Add the Zesty Flavour of Ginger

If, like me, you are a fan of fresh ginger, try adding 1–2 teaspoons grated fresh root ginger to the vinegar before bringing it to the boil.

Impress your guests with carrots coloured the incredible hue of a desert sunset. Beetroot (beet) pickling liquid is used as the blanching medium for the carrots, so no more explanations should be needed! I was inspired to make this dish when seeking out tasty colourful pickled vegetables for filling nori rolls. But since then I have been having fun adding Crimson Carrots to hot tasty noodle dishes and soups, crispy salads and vegetable platters and as a colourful garnish.

Method

Place the beetroot liquid in a small to medium-sized saucepan and bring it to the boil.

Add the carrots, ensuring that they are fully immersed in the liquid. Bring the mixture back to the boil and boil for 1–2 minutes only. (The texture should be tender crisp.)

Remove the carrots and spread them out on a platter or large plate to help them cool rapidly.

Use as required, and have fun asking people to guess what the incredible new vegetable is!

Ingredients

2 cups (500 mL/ 16 fl oz) beetroot (beet) pickling liquid

250 g (8 oz) thin carrot sticks or diced carrots, about 1 cup

Makes about 1 cup (250 g/8 oz)

Don't Throw out Beetroot (Beet) Pickling Liquid

After you have tried this recipe, I'm sure you will value the beetroot pickling liquid that, like me, you have most probably been draining down the sink for years. It will keep in a jar in the refrigerator for a week or so. When you have a moment or two, show this trick to any kids in sight.

Vibrant green florets of blanched broccoli are terrific to have on hand for vegetable platters, salads, stir-fries and snacks. Cauliflower has a lovely crunchy texture and full-bodied flavour when raw; blanching softens the strong flavour of raw cauliflower and improves both the intensity of colour and the texture of broccoli.

Method

Ingredients

1 kg (2 lb) broccoli or cauliflower coarse stalk ends trimmed

Using a small sharp knife, remove flower heads from the stalks of the broccoli (or cauliflower). Using your fingers or the knife, separate the flower heads into florets and set the stalks aside. (See the note below for using these.)

Place the broccoli (or cauliflower) florets in a heatproof bowl and completely cover with the boiling water. Allow to stand for 1 minute, then quickly and carefully drain the water off.

Plunge the florets into the icy water for 1 minute to 'refresh' them and prevent further cooking. Drain the florets and spread them out on a clean, dry tea towel to dry.

For the microwave method, place the florets in a microwave-proof dish, cover and cook on high for 1½–2 minutes.

Serves 4 Eat as soon as possible, or store the florets in an airtight container in the refrigerator for a day or two.

How to Use Broccoli and Cauliflower Stalks

Broccoli and cauliflower florets are popular but many of us forget that the stalks can be used as a vegetable in their own right. Put them in a plastic bag or container and store in the refrigerator for up to 1 week. When ready to use, simply trim the stalks and cut into cubes, slices or sticks and stir-fry in a little sesame oil with pepper to taste. Or throw them into other dishes such as soups, braises, pies and stir-fries.

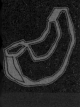

Parsnips are a grossly underrated vegetable as far as I can gather, yet whenever I serve this beautiful soup, it inspires great words of praise. Just glance at this recipe and you'll see that there are no secret or exotic ingredients — it's the true flavour of the main vegetable that makes it special. There is such a thing as beauty in simplicity.

Method

Heat the oil in a large saucepan and stir the onion over a medium heat for 1 minute. Then cover and cook for 5 minutes. (This will help soften the onion quickly and also give you a chance to prepare the parsnips.)

Add the parsnips and stir for 1 minute. Cover and cook for 10 minutes, turning down the heat so that the parsnips don't catch on the bottom of the pan. I said above that there is no secret to this recipe, but I should mention that there is a very good reason that the flavour of the parsnips is so wonderful — and it is this step of cooking them in their own steam with the lid on the pan.

Add the vegetable stock and stir the soup until it returns to the boil. Reduce the heat further and cook for 10–15 minutes, or until the parsnips are tender.

Using a food processor or blender, blend the soup with the milk until creamy smooth, using as much milk as it takes to reach the desired consistency.

Season to taste with the pepper and serve piping hot sprinkled with the parsley.

Ingredients

2–3 teaspoons oil

1–2 large onions, chopped, about 2 cups (300 g/ 10 oz)

1 kg (2 lb) parsnips, trimmed, peeled and chopped

2 cups (500 mL/16 fl oz) vegetable stock

2–3 cups (500–750 mL/ 16–24 fl oz) milk

pepper

chopped parsley to garnish

Serves 4-6

Ingredients

2–3 teaspoons oil

2 large onions, chopped, about 2 cups (300 g/ 10 oz)

2 large carrots, scrubbed or peeled and diced

2–3 celery stalks, sliced, about 2 cups (250 g/8 oz)

2–3 broccoli stalks, trimmed and sliced

2–3 garlic cloves, crushed (pressed)

1 capsicum (sweet pepper), seeded and diced, about 1½ cups (300 g/10 oz)

2–3 medium tomatoes, diced, about 2 cups (500 g/16 oz)

5 cups (1 litre/ 2 imp pints) vegetable stock

2 cups (400 g/ 14 oz) cooked or canned (tinned) beans

8 spring onions (scallions), sliced, green tops included

cracked black pepper

chopped parsley or celery leaves for garnishing

Serves 4–6

This is exactly as it sounds — all you could ever want from a warming substantial soup in one dish. This recipe is an ideal way to use up the bits and pieces of vegetables you have been collecting all week in your refrigerator. I have found that it is the perfect way to use up broccoli stalks, and since all of my family and friends love brilliant green broccoli florets over just about everything from baked jacket potatoes to hot pasta dishes, we usually collect quite a few stalks during the week. This soup is never the same, for it is rare to have exactly the same vegetable leftovers from week to week (apart from the broccoli stalks, in my case!). If you don't have any cooked or canned (tinned) red kidney beans, use cooked or canned lima or canellini beans. If you don't have these either, simply tip in a can of good old baked beans!

Delicious additions to this soup include cooked pasta (about 2 cups' worth) and freshly cooked couscous (page 119), spooned into a bowl just before ladling the soup over. (Remember not to cook the pasta for too long, or it will disintegrate.)

Method

Heat the oil in a large saucepan and stir the onion over a medium heat for 1 minute. Cover and cook over a medium heat for 5 minutes.

Then stir in the carrot, celery and broccoli and cover and cook for 5 minutes more.

Stir in the garlic, capsicum, tomato and stock and bring the soup to the boil. Reduce the heat and simmer for 15 minutes.

Stir in the beans and spring onions and season to taste with the pepper.

Serve piping hot scattered with the chopped parsley (or celery leaves).

If, like me, you are fascinated by colour, you will appreciate the brilliant hue of this tasty fat-free sauce. Use it alongside a tomato-based sauce for pasta for a colour and flavour blast. Or, reduce the amount of stock in the recipe to ½ cup (125 mL/ 4 fl oz) and use the resulting purée as a delicious dip. Or why not try one of my favourite ways to use this sauce which is to perform a Crescent Dragonwagon trick. And what is a Crescent Dragonwagon trick, you may ask. See my note below ...

Method

Cook the peas and the onion until tender by steaming in a steamer insert in a saucepan with approximately 2 cups (500 mL/16 fl oz) boiling water for about 10 minutes.

To cook in a microwave oven, place the peas and onion in a microwave ovenproof dish, cover and cook on high for 6 minutes.

Then, using a blender or food processor, blend the peas and onion until smooth with the vegetable stock and coriander.

Season to taste with the pepper and serve warm, or reheat gently, stirring.

Ingredients

250 g (8 oz) frozen green peas (not the minted variety)

¼ white onion, finely chopped, about ¼ cup (60 g/2 oz)

1 cup (250 mL/8 fl oz) vegetable stock

¼ cup chopped coriander (cilantro)

pepper

Makes about 2½ cups (625 mL/ 1 imp pint)

Who is Crescent Dragonwagon?

Crescent is a newfound friend — a passionate foodie and best-selling author who lives in the midwest United States. Look out for her best-selling *Dairy Hollow House Soup and Bread Cookbook* and I'm sure you will be inspired just as I was, for Crescent's passion for cooking and writing has won many hearts. Creative and colourful, Crescent talks about using plastic squeeze bottles (the ones used to squirt tomato sauce and mustard on to hot dogs, pies and pasties) to 'squiggle' colour on top of soups using vivid vegetable sauces and purées. I love the thought of creating edible art, for food is a wonderful artistic medium. Have fun using these squirty bottles to squiggle all types of vibrantly coloured fruit or vegetable sauces over sweet and savoury dishes alike.

I often serve these instead of deep-fried chips, which are much higher in fat. Even though these chips take longer to cook in the oven, you don't have to stand guard over them as they bake, while deep-fried chips do need to be watched constantly, and at the end of the day you have a sizeable pot of oil to dispose of! At the end of *this* recipe, you only have delicious, healthy chips.

Method

Ingredients

6 large potatoes, scrubbed

3 teaspoons oil plus a little additional oil

¼ teaspoon cracked black pepper

Serves 4–6

Preheat the oven to 220°C/425°F.

Cut the potatoes into about ½-cm (⅒-in) thick slices or 1-cm (⅕-in) thick chips, then place them in a large bowl.

Drizzle the oil over and, using your hands, rub it over the potatoes.

Arrange the chips in a single layer on a baking tray (sheet) that has been brushed with a little oil.

Bake the chips in a hot oven for 25 minutes, making sure that they are cooked inside by testing one or two with a fork and are an appetising golden-brown colour on the outside. Sprinkle on black pepper.

The Thinner they are, the Fatter they are!

This sounds like a bold contradiction, but it is quite true when it comes to deep-fried chips, for the chunkier the chip, the greater the volume of potato in ratio to its surface area. So you're eating more potato and less fat. Long slender chips such as French Fries have a much smaller volume of potato in ratio to the surface area of the chip so you're eating less potato and more fat. To take this principle one step further, it's not hard to imagine the fat or oil absorption potential of the wafer-thin variety of potato crisps!

When it comes to a quick meal, many's the time a few good-sized potatoes and a microwave oven have saved the day. Fortunately, my family and friends love potatoes, and especially enjoy the range of toppings that we have dreamed up together. We always have a ready supply of thick (Greek-style) yoghurt on hand, which we have come to use instead of sour cream due to its much lower fat content. You can, of course, use light sour cream which contains about half the fat content of regular sour cream. Combinations of shredded, chopped or diced fresh vegetables score well, as does grated tasty (mature cheddar) cheese, but go easy on the amount or this potentially healthy meal can suddenly become laden with fat. And if you choose tasty low-fat toppings and sauces, you can get away with omitting butter or margarine. There is no end to the variety of tasty toppings that can be served on top of Baked Jacket Potatoes. I have listed some of our favourite baked potato toppers below.

Method

To cook the potatoes in a microwave oven, simply prick the skins with a skewer or fork and arrange them evenly around the edge of the oven turntable. Cook on high for 10–12 minutes, then allow to stand for 2 minutes.

To cook in a conventional oven, place potatoes in a prepared oven tray and bake at 190°C/375°F for 45 minutes – 1 hour.

Split the potatoes open and serve while piping hot.

Ingredients

4 large potatoes, scrubbed

Serves 4

Baked Potato Toppers

- Fresh Tomato Salsa (page 26)
- Quick Red and Green Salsa (page 18)
- Crunchy Red Cabbage Salad (page 46)
- Avocado Hot Stuff (page 27)
- Blanched Broccoli or Cauliflower (page 34)
- Chilli Beans (page 131)
- Creamy Tofu Dip (page 153)

Popular with kids and adults alike, the aroma of these potato wedges attracts all in the vicinity. For a quick meal, begin by heating your oven, then start the wedges off by part-cooking them in a steamer or microwave oven as outlined below. This saves on cooking time; you finish the process in a conventional oven. If you have a combination microwave and convection oven, even better. When using a conventional oven for browning the wedges, you have around 20 minutes or so while the wedges are browning to whip up a range of simple toppings and a leafy salad to serve with them.

Ingredients

4 large potatoes, scrubbed

½ cup (125 mL/ 4 fl oz) yoghurt

3 garlic cloves, crushed (pressed)

1 teaspoon sweet paprika

¼ teaspoon cayenne pepper

¼ teaspoon cracked black pepper

a little oil

¼ cup chopped parsley

Serves 4

Method

Preheat the oven to 230°C/450°F.

Cut the potatoes into thick wedges, then cook them until almost tender by steaming them in a steamer insert in a saucepan with approximately 2 cups (500 mL/16 fl oz) boiling water for 10 minutes.

Or, for the microwave method, place them in a microwave-proof dish, covering and cooking them on high for 5 minutes.

When they are ready, spread the potatoes out on a tray or platter to cool for 5 minutes or so.

Meanwhile, combine the yoghurt, garlic, paprika, cayenne pepper and cracked black pepper in a large bowl.

Add the potato wedges and, using your hands, toss the wedges to ensure all are coated with the yoghurt mixture.

Arrange them in a single layer on a baking tray (sheet) that has been brushed with a little oil.

Bake the wedges in a very hot oven for 20–25 minutes, making sure that they are cooked inside by testing one or two with a fork and are an appetising golden-brown colour on the outside.

Sprinkle with the parsley and serve on a large platter or individual plates with small bowls of your choice of accompaniments (see suggestions below).

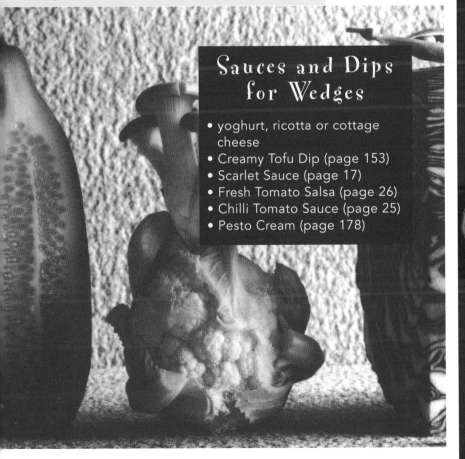

Sauces and Dips for Wedges

- yoghurt, ricotta or cottage cheese
- Creamy Tofu Dip (page 153)
- Scarlet Sauce (page 17)
- Fresh Tomato Salsa (page 26)
- Chilli Tomato Sauce (page 25)
- Pesto Cream (page 178)

The name on the seedling tag of the pansies I recently planted inspired the name for this salad. Pansies — or their edible blossoms, at least — are the star of this simple meal, but you can use other edible flowers such as cheerful nasturtiums or marigolds. Just before serving, dress Happy Faces Salad with a light tangy dressing, add some slices of small sun-ripened tomatoes, a sliver or two of a good cheese, a scattering of oven-roasted nuts and some fresh crusty bread, and you have a simple and nourishing meal.

Method

Ingredients

1 butter lettuce, washed, trimmed and torn into large bite-sized pieces, or 6 cups (200 g/ 7 oz) mixed salad greens

2–3 tablespoons finely sliced chives or spring onions (scallions), green tops included

petals of 12 or so pansies or other small edible blossoms and 2 intact blossoms for garnishing

Serves 4

Refresh the greens in cold water, then drain and dry thoroughly. I like to use a salad spinner which operates like the spin dry cycle of many washing machines — using centrifugal force to extract most of the moisture clinging to greens after washing. If, however, you do not have a salad spinner, put the greens in a clean dry pillow case or completely enclose them in a tea towel and give them a good shake out of a window or outside in the garden.

Arrange the greens on a large plate or platter and scatter the chives (or spring onions) over the greens.

Then sprinkle the salad with the petals which have been separated from the blossoms, keeping one or two blossoms intact as a garnish.

Prepare the dressing (see recipe opposite), and drizzle over the salad just as you serve it, to retain the crisp texture of the greens.

This dressing is named not only because it goes so well with the salad, but also because everyone who eats it ends up wearing a happy face. Light and tangy, it complements green salads beautifully and — joy upon joy! — it is low in fat.

Method

If using the garlic, place it in a screw-top jar and stir in the honey.

Using a fork, whisk in the vinegar, lemon (or lime) juice, pepper and oil, then shake the jar well.

Serve straightaway, or make sure you shake the dressing vigorously just before using, so that the oil and vinegar are combined well.

Ingredients

1 garlic clove, crushed (pressed) (optional)

1 scant teaspoon honey

2 tablespoons raspberry vinegar or white wine vinegar

juice of 1 lemon or lime, about 4 tablespoons

pinch of cracked black pepper

1 tablespoon olive or sunflower seed oil

Makes about ½ cup (125 mL/4 fl oz)

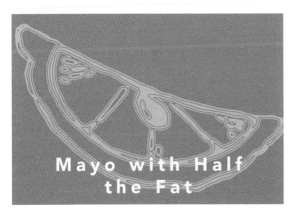

Mayo with Half the Fat

If you love the taste of mayonnaise but not the high fat content, simply mix one part mayo with one to two parts natural yoghurt. The more natural yoghurt you use, the lower in fat the dressing will be.

Include this wonderful salad in a mixed salad plate. Serve with a Mediterranean-style braised vegetable dish or use as a munchy sandwich filling. Or enjoy using it as a garnish for Baked Jacket Potatoes (page 39) by spooning it over a sour cream or yoghurt topping.

Ingredients

2 cups (180 g/6 oz) finely chopped red cabbage

2 tablespoons raspberry vinegar or red wine vinegar

1 teaspoon honey

1 beetroot (beet), trimmed, scrubbed and grated, about 1½ cups (275 g/ 9 oz)

1 crunchy red apple, skin left on, diced finely

¼ red (Spanish) onion, diced finely, about ¼ cup (60 g/2 oz)

¼ teaspoon cracked black pepper

Serves 4

Method

Place the cabbage in a medium-sized mixing bowl and sprinkle with the vinegar.

Toss the cabbage well to ensure that the vinegar is incorporated.

Drizzle the honey over, then add all the remaining ingredients and combine well.

If not serving immediately, store in a covered container in the refrigerator for up to 1 week.

Have a Ready Supply of Vinegars

Vinegar used to be brown or white. Not any more. These days we can choose from white wine, balsamic, red wine, sherry, brown rice, fruit and herb-infused vinegars. Add a slurp of balsamic vinegar to finished pasta sauces or soups, or sprinkle a little over sun-ripened strawberries before dusting them with caster sugar for a tangy surprise. Brown rice vinegar adds a real lift to stir-fry dishes and fruit and herb-infused vinegars are beautiful added to salad dressings or sprinkled over ripe tomatoes or avocados.

These are all usually available from your delicatessen or even supermarket or Asian grocery store and they keep well in a cool dark place.

This crimson wonder is stunning served as a filling for Psychedelic Sushi Rolls (page 107) and also as a garnish for Tofu Canapes (page 162). It adds a special dimension to Mountain Bread Roll-ups (page 76) too.

Method

Place the vinegar, sugar, salt and pepper in a medium-sized saucepan and bring the mixture to a boil, stirring.

Add the cabbage and boil for 2–3 minutes.

Strain the juice from the cabbage and retain.

Place the cabbage in a clean jar and, when the juice has cooled to room temperature, pour it over the cabbage.

Use at once, or store in the refrigerator for up to 1 week.

Ingredients

2 cups (500 mL/ 16 fl oz) white vinegar

2 tablespoons sugar

½ teaspoon salt

¼ teaspoon cracked black pepper

¼ small red cabbage, trimmed and shredded finely, about 4 cups (360 g/12 oz)

Makes about 4 cups (360 g/12 oz)

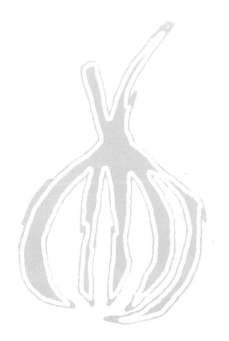

What a favourite this is, and what a sight for sore eyes! I love bringing out the brilliant hue of red cabbage, which in its raw state is a brilliant crimson anyway. But when an acid medium such as fresh lemon, lime or orange juice is tossed through it, the colour intensifies. This, combined with the rich orange of fresh carrots and the vivid green of chopped fresh chives is an incredible mix. Use this salad to add a blast of colour to a salad plate or as a crunchy munchy filling for hearty sandwiches. Use as a colourful garnish for thick soups, hotpots or Baked Jacket Potatoes (page 39).

Method

Ingredients

4 cups (360 g/ 12 oz) shredded or chopped red cabbage

juice of ½ orange or 1 lemon *or* 1 lime, about 4 tablespoons

2 medium-sized carrots, scrubbed or peeled and diced finely

¼ cup chopped chives *or* green tops of several spring onions (scallions), finely sliced

Serves 4

Place the cabbage in a bowl and drizzle the lemon (or lime or orange) juice over.

Mix well to ensure that the juice coats the cabbage. This will start the colour-intensifying process off right before your eyes!

Add the carrot and chives (or spring onions) and toss all together to combine thoroughly.

Serve at once or store in a covered container in the refrigerator for up to 2–3 days.

A Note on Chopping Cabbage

I find that using a heavy Chinese chopper makes an easy task of chopping cabbage. I like the texture of hand-chopped cabbage as many food processors chop vegetables too finely and can reduce cabbage to a pulpy mix instead of separate strands of crisp cabbage leaves. Take care, however, to thoroughly chop the thick ribs running through the leaves so that the salad has a reasonably even texture.

Vegetable platters are true sanity savers because as long as you have a platter of crisp appetising vegies ready, you can ward off hungry throngs from the kitchen while you get on with the task of preparing a quick meal. The other bonus is that a healthy snack of vegetables won't fill people up so much that they can't eat the meal you have been working hard to prepare! (The same cannot be said for biscuits, chips and hunks of cheese as a starter.) A sure-fire tip to tempt kids is to serve a nest of freshly washed, scrubbed or peeled baby carrots with their bright green leaves intact — this way 'ordinary old carrots' can be simply and quickly transformed into extra special 'Bugs Bunny carrots'!

Try making a beautiful platter using your choice of the following vegetables. You can make your platter as simple or as complicated as you wish — from a side plate of crisp carrot, celery and red capsicum (sweet pepper) sticks nestling amongst fresh greens to a more festive presentation and selection of fresh, blanched, roasted and pickled vegetables. Simply choose how far you want to go on the festive scale using the time you have available as the guide for each occasion.

Vegetables for Platters

- fresh carrots, celery, young cauliflower, capsicums (sweet peppers) and young green beans

- blanched or lightly steamed cauliflower, broccoli and green beans

- roasted sweet potatoes, pumpkin, capsicums (sweet peppers), beetroot (beets) and eggplant (aubergine)

- pickled carrots, cucumbers and cauliflower

- marinated sun-dried tomatoes, capsicums (sweet peppers) and artichoke hearts

This recipe is my version of Nori Maki, Japanese salad rolls. While Westerners traditionally eat all manner of fillings encased in bread, the Japanese fold a range of fillings in sheets of nori to form cones, parcels or rolls. Here are a few concoctions that I have found to be real winners for filling nori rolls, but enjoy thinking up your own wild and wonderful mixtures. Fresh crisp or blanched vegetables do best here, and make a refreshing lunch or snack in warmer weather. In cold weather, I tend to use more rice in the filling, with plenty of shredded pickled ginger and even a touch of chilli to warm up the body. All you basically need in the cupboard is a steady supply of white miso (see note on page 161) and wasabi paste, wonderful spread directly on to the nori sheets before the vegetables are added. Wasabi, otherwise known as Japanese horseradish, has a fantastic zingy flavour that really has the tastebuds sitting up and taking notice! (You can buy wasabi from Asian grocery stores.) The purpose of the miso or wasabi is twofold — firstly to add flavour, and secondly to help keep the vegetables adhered to the nori so that all is not lost with the first bite. Serve Salad Nori Rolls with a tasty dipping sauce if you like (see pages 52, 53). However, if you have already packed your rolls with a punch of flavour from miso or wasabi, this is a nice but unnecessary touch.

Try These Fillings Too

crisp fresh bean shoots

strips of raw or roasted capsicum
(sweet pepper)

blanched snow peas (mangetout)

shredded pickled ginger

sweet potato, peeled, cut into thin sticks
and blanched

shredded spinach or other tasty dark
leafy vegetable

roasted nuts

Method

Take one sheet of nori at a time and spread thinly with wasabi or miso.

Arrange the vegetables and fruit in rows parallel to the edge closest to you.

Using a pastry brush, brush a little warm water along the edge furthest from you.

Using firm, even pressure, roll the vegetables and fruit up in the nori, pressing the moistened far end of the nori onto the roll to secure it.

Continue with the remaining nori sheets and filling ingredients.

Using a sharp knife, cut each long roll into about 6 even slices and arrange on a serving platter or individual plates.

Daikon Radish

The daikon radish is a really wonderful vegetable which is widely used in Japanese cooking. It is an unusually long white root vegetable with a pungent flavour. I love the distinctive flavour of both fresh and pickled daikon. The golden pickled variety adds a blast of both colour and flavour to dishes based on noodles and tofu. Grated raw, it can be used as a condiment with many Asian-style dishes. To soften the flavour of fresh daikon radish in salads and stir-fries, it can be blanched. Simply peel and slice the radish into strips, then use the same method as for blanching broccoli and cauliflower (page 34). Both fresh and pickled daikon radish is available from Asian grocery stores, where you'll find varying lengths of pickled daikon are packaged in long plastic pouches. I usually buy quite a large amount, then, once the package has been opened, store the remaining pickled daikon in a screw-top jar in the refrigerator. It will keep for up to 2 weeks stored like this.

Ingredients

4 sheets toasted nori

4 teaspoons wasabi paste *or* white miso

1 carrot, scrubbed and cut into thin sticks *or* 150 g/5 oz Quick Pickled Carrots (page 32)

½ cup (150 g/5 oz) pickled daikon radish cut into thin sticks

1 avocado, peeled and sliced

½ mango, peeled and sliced (optional)

4 spring onions (scallions), sliced finely, green tops included

130 g (8 oz) mixed salad greens, chopped roughly, about 4 cups

Makes 24

Vinaigrette

Vinaigrette dressings are a combination of oil and vinegar with flavouring ingredients such pepper, paprika and garlic. Deliciously different vinaigrette can be made from flavoured vinegars such as the raspberry variety. Even puréed fruit such as mango can be whisked into a vinaigrette to impart a sweet 'nectarful' flavour to fresh seasonal greens. This popular dressing adds a splash of colour and characteristic fruity flavour to salads and vegetable dishes.

Method

Ingredients

3 tablespoons raspberry vinegar

1 tablespoon white wine vinegar

2 tablespoons olive oil

1 teaspoon honey

1 garlic clove, crushed (pressed)

pepper

Makes ½ cup
(125 mL/4 fl oz)

Place all the ingredients in a screw-top jar and shake well. Use at once, or store in the refrigerator for up to one week.

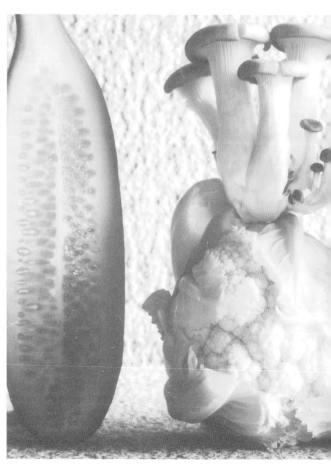

For those who appreciate a dressing that is sure to wake up even the sleepiest of taste buds. Balsamic vinegar, with its distinctive spicy tang, is the key ingredient.

Method

Place all the ingredients in a screw-top jar and shake well. Use at once, or store in the refrigerator for up to one week.

Ingredients

1–2 garlic cloves, crushed (pressed)

1 tablespoon extra virgin olive oil

1 tablespoon balsamic vinegar

4 tablespoons red wine vinegar

cracked black pepper

Makes ½ cup (125 mL/4 fl oz)

Garlic & Ginger sauce

This sauce adds a zesty flavour to any rice or noodle dish. Use it as a dipping sauce or to drizzle over steamed or blanched broccoli or any stir-fried vegetable dish.

Ingredients

2 garlic cloves, crushed (pressed)

2 teaspoons finely grated root ginger

2 teaspoons honey

3 tablespoons soy sauce

4 tablespoons apple juice

pepper

Makes about ½ cup (125 mL/4 fl oz)

Method

Place all the ingredients in a screw-top jar and shake well to combine. Use at once, or store in the refrigerator for up to one week.

This is delicious served as a dipping sauce with wedges of pita bread or with crisp vegetables. Or try it with roasted vegetables, Baked Jacket Potatoes (page 39) or Golden Potato Wedges (page 40).

Method

Ingredients

3 tablespoons chopped coriander (cilantro)

1–2 garlic cloves, crushed (pressed)

1 cup (250 mL/ 8 fl oz) yoghurt

pepper

Makes about 1 cup (250 mL/8 fl oz)

Place all the ingredients in a small mixing bowl and, using a wooden spoon, mix thoroughly.

Transfer the sauce to a serving bowl and serve at once, or cover and store in the refrigerator for 1–2 days.

A Variation Using Mint

Simply replace the coriander with 3 tablespoons chopped mint and 1 tablespoon chopped parsley. Mint and Yoghurt Sauce is delicious served with hot, spicy dishes.

Serve this light sauce with any type of sushi or nori roll or baked tofu. Great, too, for drizzling over hot or cold noodle dishes or green salads.

Method

Place all the ingredients in a screw-top jar and shake well to combine.

Use at once, or shake well again just before serving.

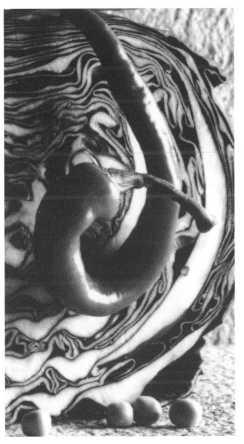

Ingredients

1 teaspoon finely sliced, seeded chillies (chilli peppers)

1 teaspoon sesame oil

2 tablespoons soy sauce

4 tablespoons apple juice *or* apricot nectar

2 tablespoons mirin

1 tablespoon finely sliced chives

cracked black pepper

Makes about ½ cup (125 mL/4 oz)

Fabulous

Fruit

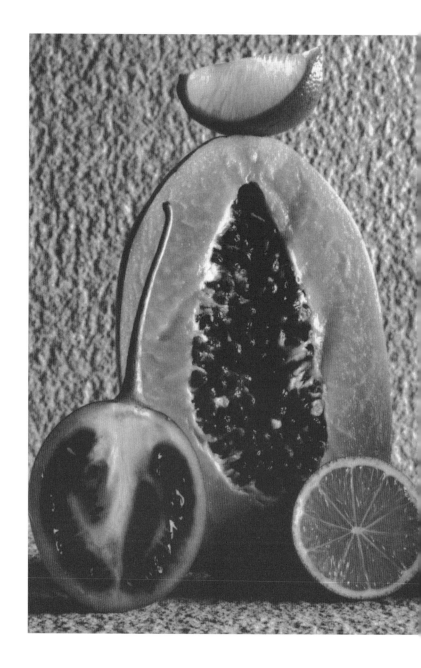

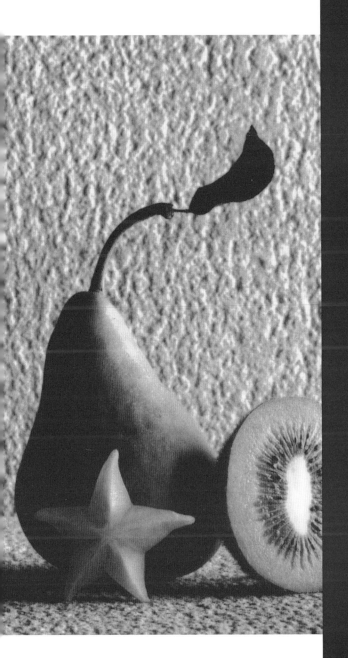

Fruit has always gladdened my heart. I'm not sure whether it's the amazing colours, the tantalising flavours or the wonderful fragrance of the best of the season's harvest that most inspires me. Biting into a beautiful juicy peach or slicing fresh mango and releasing its perfume is the best appetiser I know.

Like vegetables, fruit comes in an unbelievable range of colours, tastes and textures. Although we have to wait for the warmer months for fresh berries and beautiful stone fruits, we can look forward to what is in store for us by incorporating frozen berries, tangy berry sauces and vibrant berry vinegars in our cooking.

Even stone fruits can be savoured when we snack on dried peaches and apricots or tuck into fruits which have been canned (tinned) or home preserved in their own juice. There is no need to pile on copious quantities of sugar when flavour and sweetness can be added in the form of pure fruit juice. Sugar should be added to enhance, not drown out, the sometimes delicate natural sweetness of fruit. There are always exceptions to rules, of course, and some fruits do require more than the usual amount of sugar — quinces, gooseberries and rhubarb spring to mind immediately. Just imagine taking the new season's quinces, stewing them in apple juice or apple and blackcurrant juice to emphasise the pink blush of cooked quinces and topping off this simple dish with a dollop or two of pure cream or thick (Greek-style) yoghurt.

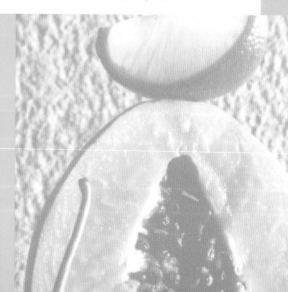

Fresh fruit is one of the best snack foods I have found, so I buy large quantities of it. To make sure it is eaten I usually prepare simple but appetising platters of seasonal fruit for friends and family. Fruit platters are especially appealing to kids as a healthy after-school snack. They are also wonderful served as an appetiser before meals, as a weekend or holiday breakfast or brunch and as a refreshing dessert or supper. Use fresh seasonal fruit wherever possible, and top up with fruit canned (tinned) in its own juice and dried fruits. Turn the page for some colourful and delicious combinations.

To Prepare Pineapples

Using a sharp serrated stainless steel knife, remove the top of the pineapple and cut the fruit in half crossways. Place the pineapple halves, cut side down, on a chopping board and shave the skin off using the sharp knife, taking care to remove the 'eyes' from the flesh. Cut the pineapple into wedges, slices or large cubes.

To Prepare Mangoes

Wash the fruit and, leaving the skin on, cut from top to bottom close to the pip, to obtain two plump 'cheeks'.. Using a small sharp knife, make lengthways and crossways cuts into the mango flesh, taking care not to pierce the skin. Turn the mango almost inside-out to fan out the flesh in a decorative manner. For peeling and slicing mangoes, if not over-ripe, use a vegetable peeler to remove the skin, then, using a sharp stainless steel knife, cut from top to bottom close to the pip as above. Dice or slice and use as required.

To Prepare Pawpaw (Papaya)

Wipe over the pawpaw with a clean damp cloth, then peel, using a vegetable peeler if the fruit is still firm, or a small sharp knife if the fruit is ripe and soft. Cut the pawpaw in half lengthways and, using a teaspoon, remove the pips, taking care not to remove too much flesh. Using a sharp knife, cut the pawpaw into neat slices or large cubes.

Spring

Spring is the perfect time for show-casing beautiful tropical fruits such as pineapples, mangoes and pawpaw (papaya) which are ideal served simply. Prepare and arrange the fruit on a platter just before serving. Garnish with edible blossoms or herbs and serve with lime or lemon wedges.

Summer

Summer is the best time for preparing fruit platters because of the bountiful supply of quality fresh fruits available. And fruit tempts jaded appetites in hot weather. Select a good variety, but take care not to overdo it or you may end up with an over-cluttered platter.

Choose halved stone fruits, whole berries and cherries and wedges of honeydew melon, rock melon (cantaloupe) and watermelon. Beautiful garnishes for festive summer platters include clumps of redcurrants, whole strawberries with the bright green hulls left on or whole lychees (with a cross cut into their skins at the top so that they can be peeled back to reveal the luscious translucent flesh).

Autumn

Figs and grapes are the bounty of autumn, and look good in edible arrangements. If you can obtain fig or grape leaves these make an interesting backdrop for a special festive platter. You may be able to add a last taste of summer with a mound of autumn raspberries, or try a touch of the exotic by adding wedges of ripe persimmon. Whole nuts like walnuts and almonds add another dimension; arrange a mound of nuts in the centre of the platter, and serve with a nutcracker nearby.

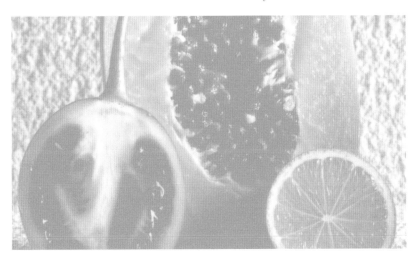

Winter

It's a shame that fruit is often neglected in the winter months, but it can provide a refreshing change to the warming winter dishes we base our meals on. Apples, nashi (Asian pears), kiwifruit (Chinese gooseberries), oranges and mandarins are in season during this time and can be sliced and arranged attractively on a platter. For variety, top up with pineapple, apricots, nectarines or peaches which have been home preserved or canned (tinned) in their own juice. Dried fruit such as dried apricots, peaches, dates and figs can also add contrast and an interesting variation in texture to winter fruit platters.

Fruity Blissballs

These are good to serve as a snack or an after-dinner treat, especially nestling amidst a colourful fresh fruit platter. They can be put together fresh and dried fruits, ricotta cheese, cream cheese or tofu, sweetened with honey and thickened with muesli, almond meal or desiccated (shredded) coconut.

Ingredients

250 g (8 oz) dried apricots, chopped, about 2 cups

2–3 tablespoons honey

250 g (8 oz) light cream cheese, or ricotta cheese or tofu

1 cup (115 g/4 oz) plain untoasted muesli

1 cup (90 g/3 oz) desiccated (shredded) coconut

Makes about 18

Method

Place all the ingredients, except for ½ cup of the desiccated coconut, in a large bowl and, using your hands, mix them all well using a 'squishing' action.

You should aim for a mixture with a soft dough (batter-like) consistency. Form this mixture into balls about the size of a walnut.

Place the remaining coconut into another large bowl.

When you have made 4 or 5 blissballs, roll them in the coconut and then assemble in a serving bowl or on a platter.

Continue with the rest of the mixture until all the blissballs are made.

Serve at once or store in an airtight container in the refrigerator for up to 1 week.

Blissballs freeze well, so if you want to prepare a quantity of these ahead of time or you will not use this quantity within the week, place them in a freezer bag and freeze them for up to 2 months.

Method

Prepare as outlined in the recipe for Apricot Blissballs on the previous page.

Ingredients

2 ripe bananas, mashed

juice of ½ lemon, about
2 tablespoons

2 cups (220 g/8 oz) chopped pitted (stoned) dates

1 cup (110 g/4 oz) plain untoasted muesli

⅔ cup (60 g/2 oz) desiccated (shredded) coconut

Makes about 18

Chopping Dried Apricots

Dried apricots can be chopped using a large sharp knife or a food processor with the metal blade attachment. When using a knife, try brushing the blade with a little oil because this will prevent the apricots sticking to the blade. When using a food processor, turn the processor on first, then add the apricots because this helps prevent them becoming caught on the blades.

Banana & Date Blissballs

61

Apples,

one of the most common of fruits, are good to eat just as they are — fresh and crisp and eaten whole as a very portable snack, or sliced and served with a sharp cheese for an after-dinner treat. Stewed apples are a valuable commodity in the busy person's refrigerator for they can be whipped up into crunchy crumbles, added to the morning's breakfast cereal or served with thick (Greek-style) yoghurt and a fine drizzling of honey. This recipe does not contain cane sugar, but is sweetened by the apple juice which is used in place of traditional syrups.

Method

Ingredients

4 Granny Smith apples, peeled, cored and sliced thickly

2 cups (500 mL/ 16 fl oz) apple juice

2 or 3 lemon slices

Serves 4

Place the apples in a medium-sized saucepan and add the apple juice and lemon slices.

Cover and bring to the boil, then reduce the heat and cook gently for 10 minutes, or until the apples are tender.

Soft Butter Trick

If you like the flavour of butter but are concerned about saturated fat in your diet, you can buy dairy blends which are a combination of butter and mono-unsaturated or polyunsaturated oil. Or you can whip up your very own soft version of dairy blend in minutes. This way, you also have control over the proportion of butter and oil you use. And because you can spread this mixture much more thinly on bread than regular butter, you actually use less butter per slice of bread. So, you can still have your butter and eat it too!

Simply cut 250 g (8 oz) butter into large cubes and place in a microwave-proof dish and cook on medium low for 30 seconds. Check the softness of the butter (it should be soft enough to cream, yet not melted) and continue heating in the microwave for bursts of 20 seconds until the butter is soft.

If you don't have a microwave, place the cubes of butter in a heatproof bowl and stand it in a sink of hot water, mixing occasionally until the butter becomes soft. Then, using a balloon whisk or a wooden spoon, beat the butter until it is creamy, and then beat in 2–3 tablespoons canola oil. Transfer the butter to an airtight container and store it in the pantry in cooler weather, or in the refrigerator during summer.

These 'flans' are assembled on English-style muffins rather than pastry cases which are high in fat and sometimes added sugar as well. Serve them for a special breakfast, brunch or afternoon tea.

Method

Cut the muffins in half and spread each half with cream cheese.

Carefully spread a layer of jam over the top.

Arrange the strawberries, cut side downwards, on the muffins.

Ingredients

4 English-style muffins

3–4 tablespoons cream cheese

3 tablespoons strawberry jam (jelly)

1 punnet (carton) strawberries, halved, hulls removed

Makes 8

Quick Apricot 'Flans'

In this recipe apricots are offset beautifully by the green translucent flesh of kiwifruit. Top with a ripe red strawberry with the vibrant green hull attached for a special treat.

Method

Ingredients

4 English-style muffins

3–4 tablespoons cream cheese

3 tablespoons apricot jam (jelly)

16 fresh or canned apricot halves (one 825 g/2 lb tin)

2 kiwifruit (Chinese gooseberries), peeled and cut into crossways slices

Makes 8

Cut the muffins in half and spread each half with cream cheese.

Carefully spread a layer of jam over the top.

If using canned (tinned) apricots, drain them thoroughly.

Arrange the apricot halves and the kiwifruit on the muffins.

63

Designed

Designed by my son Des who one day exclaimed, 'Let's make Apple Pizza instead of Apple Pie!' So, thanks to Des, we now have a delicious spicy apple pizza recipe in our repertoire. And what wisdom children have — for pizza dough (batter) contains only a trace of fat instead of the copious amounts required in standard pastry recipes.

Ingredients

Crust

¾ cup (185 mL/ 6 fl oz) hot water

2 teaspoons sugar

¾ cup (185 mL/ 6 fl oz) low-fat milk or cold water

7 g (¼ oz) active dried yeast

1½ cups (185 g/ 6 oz) unbleached white flour

1 cup (155 g/5 oz) wholemeal (wholewheat) flour

additional flour

Topping

3 tablespoons apple jelly

4–6 large Granny Smith apples, peeled, cored and sliced

2 tablespoons melted butter

3 tablespoons brown sugar

1 teaspoon ground cinnamon

Makes 1 large or 2 medium pizzas

Method

Preheat the oven to 220°C/425°F.

Place the hot water in a bowl and whisk in the sugar, using a fork.

Add the milk (or cold water), then whisk in the yeast. Set the mixture aside for a few minutes to allow the yeast to start growing.

Then place the flours in a large bowl, combine thoroughly and make a 'well' in the centre.

Add the yeast mixture to the well and mix the flour in gradually until a soft dough (batter) is formed.

Turn the dough out onto your bench top which has been liberally sprinkled with some of the additional flour. Knead the dough for 1–2 minutes, then roll out to fit one large or two medium pizza trays.

Using a pastry brush, brush the apple jelly over the dough, then arrange the apple slices on top.

Using a clean pastry brush, brush the apple slices with the melted butter, then sprinkle with the sugar and dust with the cinnamon.

Bake in a hot oven for 20–25 minutes.

Serve hot or cold.

This favourite English dish traditionally contains suet — not a favourite food of vegetarians! (Suet is the solid fat that surrounds the internal organs of animals.) I have used butter or margarine and yoghurt instead of suet and have been able to achieve a pudding with a moist texture yet less saturated fat. With its cheeky name, this is a sure-fire conversation starter, so it is a fabulous dessert to serve when entertaining.

Please don't be discouraged by the lengthy cooking time. Simply plan to make it while you are at home doing other things, for it does not require close attention when cooking. Serve each slice of Spotted Dick surrounded by a berry coulis or sauce (see Fresh Strawberry Sauce on page 71).

Method

Place the flour, salt and butter (or margarine) in a food processor and process the mixture until it resembles fresh breadcrumbs.

Transfer the mixture to a mixing bowl and add the currants and sugar.

Mix well to combine the ingredients thoroughly, then make a 'well' in the centre of the mixture.

Combine the yoghurt, honey and vanilla and pour this mixture into the 'well', mixing the ingredients thoroughly until a stiff dough (batter) is formed.

Transfer the dough to a pudding basin that has been brushed with a little melted butter or margarine.

Cover tightly with a lid, or with aluminium foil folded over the top of the basin.

Immerse the basin in 3 cm (1 in) boiling water in a large pan. Cover, and steam the pudding for 2 hours, adding more water to the pan if necessary, to prevent it boiling dry.

Ingredients

2 cups (250 g/8 oz) wholemeal (wholewheat) self-raising flour

pinch of salt

90 g (3 oz) butter or margarine and additional melted butter or margarine

2½ cups (410 g/14½ oz) dried currants

½ cup (85 g/2½ oz) soft brown sugar

½ teaspoon bicarbonate of soda

1 cup natural yoghurt

3 tablespoons honey

1 teaspoon pure vanilla essence

Serves 10–12

A breeze to prepare when you have preserved or canned (tinned) apricots or peaches, some almonds and brown sugar in your pantry. Great served with a dollop of thick (double) cream or a spoonful of thick (Greek-style) yoghurt.

Method

Ingredients

½ teaspoon oil

2 cups (225 g/8 oz) fresh or canned (one 825 g/2 lb tin) and drained apricot halves *or* peach slices

½ cup (85 g/3 oz) almonds *or* hazelnuts

2–3 tablespoons brown sugar

1 teaspoon ground cinnamon

Serves 4

Preheat the oven to 190°C/375°F.

Using a pastry brush, brush the base of a heatproof dish with the oil, then arrange the apricot halves (or peach slices) on top.

Using a food processor with the metal chopping blade, chop the almonds (or hazelnuts) until a coarse meal is produced.

Add the sugar and cinnamon to the processor and process for 5 or 10 seconds only.

Sprinkle the almond mixture over the fruit and bake in a moderately hot oven for 15–20 minutes, or until the crumble topping is golden-brown.

These parfaits can be easily assembled from fresh seasonal fruits with yoghurt and a scoop of ice cream if you like. They need never be boring if you follow the cycle of the seasons, for even in winter, these delectable parfaits can feature diced or sliced fresh apples or stewed apples such as Apples in their Own Juice (page 62). Even iced oranges go well with yoghurt and a drizzling of honey because this combination results in a delicious sherbet-flavoured parfait. For greater variety when fresh fruits are limited, use fruit which has been canned (tinned) in its own juice, and chopped or sliced dried fruits such as figs, apricots and dates.

Method

To Assemble Parfaits

Simply use alternate layers of several of the listed ingredients to fill tall glasses. Top with sliced fresh or dried fruit and a drizzling of honey.

whole fresh berries, grapes and cherries

sliced fresh fruit such as mango, pawpaw (papaya), pineapple and kiwifruit (Chinese gooseberries)

canned (tinned) fruit such as apricots, nectarines, peaches, pineapple, pears or fruit salad

sliced or chopped dried fruits such as figs, dates, raisins and apricots

chopped nuts such as almonds, hazelnuts or macadamias (for roasting nuts, see note on page 108)

fruit pulp or purées such as passionfruit (purple granadilla)

Fresh Strawberry Sauce (page 71) or Raspberry Honey (page 68)

low-fat toasted muesli or granola

fruit or natural (plain) yoghurt

a little ice cream

Figs with Raspberry Honey

Autumn is the time to savour the flavour of plump sun-ripened figs with their sweet juicy flesh. Figs harmonise well with raspberries, which is very timely because raspberries often have an autumn harvest. Even if fresh raspberries are unavailable, frozen berries can be used successfully in Raspberry Honey. Yoghurt, with its characteristic tangy edge, makes a great accompaniment.

Ingredients

8 large juicy figs

1 quantity Raspberry Honey (see below)

625 mL (1 imp pint) natural (plain) yoghurt

Serves 4

Method

Using a clean damp cloth, wipe over the figs. Snip any remaining stem section from the tops of the figs using sharp kitchen scissors.

Cut the figs in half lengthways and arrange four halves on each plate, or arrange all the figs on one large platter.

If you have a fig tree or can get hold of some fresh fig leaves, serve the figs on these for special occasions.

Spoon the Raspberry Honey over the figs and serve with a pot of yoghurt.

Raspberry Honey

A quick concoction to add a blast of ruby red to freshly cooked scones and pancakes. And a great way to add a further burst of colour to Exploding Raspberry Bread (page 70). Raspberry Honey looks fabulous served in a small pot on an underplate with a dessert spoon for serving and a blossom or two beside it.

Ingredients

½ cup (80 g/3 oz) fresh or frozen raspberries

4 tablespoons mild-flavoured honey

Makes about ½ cup (125 mL/4 fl oz)

Method

Place the berries in a small bowl and drizzle honey over them.

Mix carefully to avoid breaking up the raspberries completely.

This simple recipe is perfect for weekend breakfasts and brunches when you just want to relax and read or bask in the dappled sunlight in your garden, courtyard or balcony. Or try serving it for dessert dusted with a little icing (confectioner's) sugar and fresh berries.

Method

Using a food processor or blender, blend all the ingredients, except for the raspberries, until smooth.

Transfer the mixture to a bowl and carefully stir in the fruit.

Add a full tablespoon of the mixture to a frying pan (skillet) and cook the pancakes until golden-brown. Allow about 1 minute for the first side (2 minutes if using frozen berries), then 30 seconds for the second side. Flip the pancakes over when the bubbles rise and burst, as you would when making plain pancakes.

Enjoy at once either plain, or with Raspberry Honey, a simple ruby red concoction (see opposite).

Or allow to cool and serve dusted with a little icing (confectioner's) sugar and fresh berries.

A Note on Mild-flavoured Honeys

Orange blossom, clover or wildflower are beautiful honeys to use for Raspberry Honey (see previous page). Avoid using leatherwood or gum honeys which are a little overpowering in flavour to successfully complement berries.

Ingredients

1 cup (155 g/5 oz) wholemeal (wholewheat) flour

½ cup (55 g/2 oz) unbleached white flour

3 teaspoons baking powder

1 tablespoon caster (superfine) sugar

1 egg

1 cup (250 mL/ 8 fl oz) milk

½ teaspoon vanilla essence (extract)

1 cup (155 g/5 oz) fresh or frozen raspberries

Makes about 12 pancakes

What a treat — a luscious bread that is brimming with berries and low in fat at the same time. Moist and fruity as it is, there's no need to pile on butter either! Serve as it is, or with a little light cream cheese for spreading and some seasonal fruits. It also makes a delicious dessert served straight from the oven in all its explosive glory, with a good dollop of thick (double) cream. If you have a sweet tooth, add 1 cup (155 g/5 oz) dried currants to the batter before placing it in the tin. Serve with a pot of wildflower or orange blossom honey for drizzling. To add both sweetness and colour to your life, you can't go wrong if you serve it with a pot of Raspberry Honey (see page 68).

Method

Ingredients

1 cup (250 mL/ 8 fl oz) boiling water

4 tablespoons soft brown sugar

1 cup (250 mL/8 fl oz) milk

10 g (⅓ oz) active dried yeast

a little melted butter _or_ oil

1½ cups (250 g/ 8 oz) wholemeal (wholewheat) self-raising flour

1 cup (115 g/4 oz) unbleached white flour

1½ punnets (cartons) raspberries

Place the water in a large heatproof bowl and whisk in 1 tablespoon of the sugar, using a fork.

Add the milk, then whisk in the yeast. Set the mixture aside for 5 minutes, to allow the yeast to start growing.

Meanwhile, using a pastry brush, brush a 24-cm (4-in) square cake tin (pan) with a little melted butter or oil, and preheat the oven to 220°C/425°F.

Gradually add the flours to the yeast mixture, beating the mixture with a wooden spoon until a thick elastic dough (batter) is produced; this should only take 1 minute.

Scrape the dough into the prepared tin and smooth the top over.

Sprinkle the raspberries over the top. It is not necessary to do this in a neat even layer — in fact, a better, more explosive, crater-like effect during baking is achieved by creating a somewhat uneven layer of berries.

Sprinkle the remaining 3 tablespoons of sugar over and set the bread aside in a warm part of your kitchen for 15 minutes to prove (rise).

Bake in a hot oven until cooked through when tested with a skewer — about 25 minutes.

Makes 1 loaf

Serve hot or cold.

This sauce is so delectable that it is surprising to find how easy it is to whip up — and in minutes too! Serve generous spoonfuls over thick (Greek-style) yoghurt or ice cream, but the pièce de résistance is to spoon it over piping hot pancakes or hot crispy waffles.

Method

Warm the honey by placing it in a cup and heating in a microwave oven on medium-high for 30 seconds, or stand the cup in a heatproof bowl containing a little boiling water.

Stir in the lemon juice.

Halve or slice the strawberries, or, if they are small, leave them whole.

Place them in a bowl and drizzle the honey and lemon mixture over.

Serve at once or store in the refrigerator for a few days.

Ingredients

2 tablespoons clover *or* wildflower honey

juice of half a lemon, about 2 tablespoons

1 punnet (carton) ripe strawberries, washed and hulled

strawberry leaves *or* lemon wedges for garnishing

Makes about 2 cups (500 mL/16 fl oz)

A Note on Using Frozen Berries

Frozen raspberries can be used instead of fresh berries in many recipes, for example, in Exploding Raspberry Bread, opposite. When using frozen berries. I recommend thawing them to room temperature while the yeast mixture has been set aside. Topping the yeast dough (batter) with still frozen berries slows down the action of the yeast in the dough, and you will have to set the assembled bread aside to prove (rise) for longer (20–25 minutes).

To speed up the process of berry thawing, place the berries in a microwave-proof bowl and microwave for 3 minutes on the defrost setting. If you don't have a microwave oven, place the berries in a heatproof pottery bowl and place it in your sink so that hot water comes halfway up the sides of the bowl. (A note of caution with the sink method for the uninitiated— be careful not to turn on the tap and drown the berries, and tell all others in the household to beware also!)

Brilliant

Breads & Cereals

Thank goodness there's more to bread than white sliced! Like vegetables and fruits, breads and cereals are highly recommended foods because of the complex carbohydrate and dietary fibre they contain. And, unlike pastry dishes, bread is low in fat, that is, unless you spread it with generous amounts of butter or margarine.

The bread recipes in this book make use of tasty vegetable fillings and so do not require fatty spreads to keep them moist.

Enjoy building up any number of substantial meals from the many varieties of breads that are available these days. Watch out for mountain bread, otherwise known as sorj or lavash. As with pita pockets and souvlaki, you can roll up taste-tempting fillings inside it. And don't forget French breadsticks cut into slices or portions, bagels, buns and rolls for hearty servings. Once you add tantalising fillings created from fresh seasonal produce and sun-dried, pickled or marinated vegetables (available from most supermarkets and fresh produce stores), you'll never think of sandwiches as boring again.

When dreaming up new sandwich treats, imagine a sandwich brimming with contrasts in colour, taste and texture. Then think of which of your favourite fresh greens to add and a filling ingredient that will make the sandwich substantial and satisfying.

Breads

Serve this delicious crisp bread as an interesting accompaniment to soups and stews, with dips or on cheese platters. Try creating your own taste sensations by varying the topping ingredients.

Method

Preheat the oven to 180°C/350°F.

Brush each slice of bread lightly with the oil, then, if you wish, using kitchen scissors, cut the bread into desired shapes. (Brushing a large slice of bread with oil before cutting it is less fiddly and helps keep the amount of oil needed to a minimum.)

Sprinkle the paprika (or herbs or sesame seeds) on top.

Spread a single layer of the bread out on baking trays (sheets) and bake in a moderate oven for 15–20 minutes.

If not using that day, store the bread in an airtight container; it will keep for several days.

Ingredients

2 slices mountain (lavash or sorj) bread

flavoured oil such as chilli oil *or* garlic oil

1 teaspoon ground sweet paprika *or* dried herbs *or* sesame seeds

The tender crisp texture of the vegetable sticks in this recipe add a wonderful character to this sandwich. Peanut (groundnut) butter is used both to provide a scrumptious flavour and to ensure that the filling ingredients adhere to the bread — very practical when you are actually eating this tasty treat!

Method

Ingredients

1 teaspoon peanut (groundnut) *or* sesame oil

1 good-sized carrot, scrubbed or peeled and cut into thin sticks

2 zucchini (courgettes), trimmed and cut into thin sticks

1 capsicum (sweet pepper), seeded and cut into thin strips, about 1½ cups (300 g/10 oz)

4 spring onions (scallions), sliced finely, green tops included

1–2 garlic cloves, crushed (pressed)

1 teaspoon grated ginger (optional)

3 tablespoons vegetable stock *or* water

4 slices mountain (lavash or sorj) bread

6 teaspoons peanut (groundnut) butter

Serves 2–4 for lunch, 4 as a starter

Brush a wok or frying pan (skillet) with the oil and heat over a medium heat.

Add the carrot and stir-fry for 1 minute, then cover and cook for 2–3 minutes.

Add the zucchini and capsicum and stir over the heat for a few minutes.

Next, add the spring onions, garlic and, if using, the ginger and stir over the heat for 1 minute.

Add the vegetable stock (or water) and cover and cook for 2 minutes. The vegetables should still be tender crisp. Remember that the entire length of cooking time required will depend on how thinly you have cut the vegetables.

Set the vegetables aside to cool slightly.

Spread the bread evenly with the peanut butter, then arrange a generous strip of the vegetable filling along the end of the bread closest to you.

Using firm, even pressure, roll the bread up to enclose the filling in a cylindrical shape.

Serve at once, or cut into neat slices for a more elegant dish.

Soft and moist, this pizza is manageable to eat when rolled up and sliced. Experiment with wild and wonderful toppings to add, because this recipe can be changed to suit almost any palate.

Method

First, preheat your oven to 200°C/400°F if you are not following the microwave version of this recipe.

Combine the chopped tomato or pasta sauce and the tomato paste, then spread the mixture evenly on the bread.

Scatter the grated cheese over, then sprinkle with the spring onions, capsicum and capers (or olives).

Place the pizzas on a baking tray (sheet) and bake for 15 minutes or until the cheese has melted completely.

For the microwave version, place the pizzas on serving plates and cook one by one on high for 2 minutes.

Remove from the oven and allow to stand for a minute or two to cool slightly.

Carefully roll the pizza up in a cylindrical fashion and eat straightaway. Or, using a sharp knife, cut into neat lengths.

A Note on Warming Pita and Souvlaki Bread

To warm the bread, place it in an ovenproof dish, cover and bake at 190°C/375°F for 5 minutes. For the microwave version, place the bread on the turntable and cook on high for 1 minute. Remove the bread and wrap it in one or two clean tea towels to keep it moist and warm until you are ready to assemble the roll-ups.

Ingredients

3 ripe tomatoes, peeled and chopped, about ¾ cup (185 g/6 oz) or ¾ cup premade pasta sauce

1 tablespoon tomato paste (purée)

4 large rounds of pita or souvlaki bread

2 cups (240 g/8 oz) grated tasty (mature cheddar) cheese

4 spring onions (scallions), sliced finely, green tops included

1 capsicum (sweet pepper), seeded and diced or shredded finely, about 1½ cups (300 g/10 oz)

1 tablespoon drained pickled capers or 4 tablespoons chopped black (ripe) or stuffed green olives

Serves 4

This recipe is like an old pair of slippers — always convenient and comfortable. Yet it need not be boring. Dress it up one or two of your favourite toppings (see below).

Method

Ingredients

4 generous slices good-quality bread

125 g (4 oz) tasty (mature cheddar) cheese, sliced

pepper

Serves 2

Preheat your grill (broiler) and toast one side of the bread until golden-brown.

Turn the bread over and arrange the cheese on top.

Grill (broil) until the cheese has melted, then dust with pepper.

Serve at once with one or several toppings.

Toppings for Cheese on Toast

Scarlet Sauce (page 17)

Quick Red and Green Salsa (page 18)

Ruby Red Salad (page 44)

Quick Tomato Chutney (page 24)

Crunchy Red Cabbage Salad (page 46)

Toast is a great standby for those extra busy times when you need to eat quickly and don't want to spend more than 10 minutes whipping up a quick but satisfying snack. Toast is good for health reasons too, as long as you don't pile on the butter or margarine. For a more substantial snack or light meal, choose a good-quality wholemeal or multi-grain bread, which is also more nutritious than white bread.

Once you have toasted one or both sides of the bread, simply top with one or more of the following ingredients:

■
thin slices of feta cheese topped with thickly sliced ripe tomatoes, sliced spring onions (scallions) and cracked black pepper;

■
Roasted Capsicums (page 16) or Roasted Eggplant (Aubergine) Rounds (page 21), if you have some stacked away in your refrigerator, with tasty (mature cheddar) cheese melted on top;

■
a tasty home-made or commercially prepared dip such as houmus (page 130), spread thickly on the toast, then topped with chopped greens and fresh tomato slices;

■
mashed or sliced avocado with a squeeze of lemon or lime juice and cracked black pepper;

■
left-over cooked tofu such as Tofu Chilli Bake (page 158) or Baked Tofu Satay Slices (page 156) grilled (broiled) to reheat, then topped with shredded spinach or rocket (arugula) or lettuce.

Pesto Pizza

The full-bodied flavour of pesto makes this a really popular pizza with my family and friends.

Ingredients

1 quantity Foccacia
Dough (batter)
(opposite page)

½ cup (125 mL/
4 fl oz) Pesto Sauce
(page 92)

250 g (8 oz)
mozzarella cheese,
sliced

6 spring onions
(scallions), sliced,
green tops included

1 red capsicum
(sweet pepper),
seeded and diced,
about 1½ cups
(300 g/10 oz)

½ yellow or green
capsicum (sweet
pepper), seeded
and sliced, about
¾ cup (150 g/5 oz)

½ cup (75 g/2½ oz)
pitted (stoned)
black (ripe) olives,
halved

2 cups (250 g/
8 oz) sliced
mushrooms

Makes 1 large or 2
medium pizzas

Method

Preheat the oven to 200°C/400°F.

Brush one large or two medium-sized pizza trays (sheets).

Roll the dough out thinly to fit the trays and trim the edges.

Using a pastry brush, spread the Pesto Sauce evenly over the dough.

Arrange the cheese slices on top, then scatter with the remaining ingredients.

Bake the pizza for 10 minutes, then reduce the heat to 190°C/375°F and bake for a further 15–20 minutes to ensure the vegetables are cooked without burning the crust.

A Note on Using Self-raising Flour

I often use the self-raising variety of one of the flours in yeast doughs (batters) when they only need proving (rising) once. It seems to help make the bread lighter and fluffier than when using plain (all-purpose) flour.

Active Dried Yeast

This is great to have on hand for whipping up quick breads and pizza dough. It has been preserved whilst very fresh and active so that you should achieve good rising qualities.

This is probably the bread I make most frequently these days. Fortunately, it is very quick and easy to make, only needing one proving (rising). I usually whip up several loaves of foccacia whenever I make a pizza with a yeast dough (batter) base. This is because the recipe I use for both foccacia and pizza doughs is exactly the same. Rejoice in any left-over herbed foccacia because it makes great toasted sandwiches and a lovely base for cheese on toast.

Method

Preheat the oven to 220°C/425°F.

Place the boiling water in a heatproof bowl and whisk in the sugar.

Stir in the cold water, sprinkle the yeast over the top then whisk the yeast through the water using a fork. Set this mixture aside for a few minutes.

Meanwhile, sift the flours and salt into a large bowl. Make a 'well' in the centre and add the yeast mixture.

Gradually work enough flour into the yeast mixture to make a soft dough (batter).

Turn the dough out on to a floured board or bench top and knead vigorously for 2 minutes.

Cut the dough into two or three even pieces, knead each one lightly for a few seconds and form each piece into a long oval shape.

Use a rolling pin to roll the dough out to a 1½-cm (½-in) thickness, or simply press down with the flats of your hands.

Brush two or three baking trays (sheets) with a little of the oil and carefully transfer the foccacia to the trays.

Set aside to prove (rise) for 15–20 minutes or so.

Just before baking, brush the tops with the remaining olive oil and sprinkle the mixed herbs over.

Bake for 20–25 minutes.

Ingredients

1 cup (250 mL/ 8 fl oz) boiling water

1 teaspoon sugar

1¼ cups (300mL/ 10 fl oz) cold water

15 g (½ oz) active dried yeast

2 cups (250 g/8 oz) unbleached white flour

1½ cups (250 g/8 oz) wholemeal (wholewheat) self-raising flour

pinch of salt

additional flour

2 teaspoons olive oil

3 tablespoons dried mixed herbs

Makes 2 standard-sized or 3 small foccacias

The enticing yeasty aroma of freshly baked bread is a sure way to whet the appetite and these muffins have all the attributes of fresh bread, but can be whipped up quickly while your meal is cooking.

Method

Ingredients

¾ cup (225 mL/7 fl oz) boiling water

1–2 teaspoons raw sugar

1¼ cups (300 mL/10 fl oz) skim milk

10 g (⅓ oz) active dried yeast

1 cup (155 g/5 oz) wholemeal (wholewheat) flour

1 cup (125 g/4 oz) unbleached white flour

¾ cup (90 g/ 3 oz) multi-grain mix (available at health food stores)

2 tablespoons gluten flour

pinch of salt

Makes about 12 rolls

Preheat the oven to 220°C/425°F.

Place the water in a large mixing bowl and stir in the sugar, then add the milk.

Sprinkle the yeast on top and, using a wooden spoon, stir it in briefly. Allow the mixture to stand for about 5 minutes until a foam appears on top.

Sift the remaining ingredients into the mixture and, using a wooden spoon, mix thoroughly.

Continue beating the mixture for 1 minute, then place large spoonfuls of it into muffin tins (pans) that have been brushed with a little melted butter or margarine.

Place the muffins in a warm location for 20–25 minutes to allow them to almost double in size, then cook them in a hot oven for 20–25 minutes or until they are golden-brown and give a hollow sound when tapped on the bottom.

Gluten Flour

The addition of gluten flour helps strengthen the dough (batter). This step replaces the rather lengthy one of a considerable amount of kneading to develop the gluten component of the wholemeal and unbleached white flours in the recipe. Gluten is the protein component of the flour and helps make doughs elastic and strong when beaten. You can buy gluten in the health food section of supermarkets or at health food stores.

Moist and juicy, these muffins are low in fat and added sugar, yet are beautifully moist and sweet. They are delicious both served steaming hot straight from the oven and cold. To dress up for a sweet treat after dinner, dust the tops lightly with a little pure icing (confectioner's) sugar and serve with some fresh fruit.

Method

Preheat the oven to 220°C/425°F.

Place the water in a large mixing bowl and stir in the sugar, then add the milk.

Sprinkle the yeast on top and, using a wooden spoon, stir it in briefly. Allow the mixture to stand for about 5 minutes until a foam appears.

Sift the flour, sugar, salt and spices into the mixture and mix thoroughly.

Beat the mixture with the wooden spoon for 1 minute, then beat in the apple and sultanas.

Place large spoonfuls of the mixture into muffin pans (tins) that have been brushed with a little melted butter or margarine.

Place the muffins in a warm location for 20–25 minutes to allow them to almost double in size.

Cook in a hot oven for 20–25 minutes or until they are golden-brown and give a hollow sound when tapped on the bottom.

Try Apricot 'Cakes' as a Variation

When preparing the muffin mixture, leave out the apple and sultanas (golden raisins). Spoon into 12 greased muffin pans (tins), top with apricots (fresh in summer, or, in winter, canned (tinned) in their own juice, drained) and sprinkle with a little soft brown sugar. Bake as for Apple & Sultana Muffins.

Ingredients

½ cup (125 mL/4 fl oz) boiling water

2 teaspoons raw sugar

1 cup (250 mL/ 8 fl oz) skim milk

10 g (⅓ oz) active dried yeast

1½ cups (185 g/6 oz) wholemeal (wholewheat) flour

2 tablespoons gluten flour

1–2 tablespoons soft brown sugar

pinch of salt

3 teaspoons mixed spice

1 large Granny Smith apple, skin left on, cut into large dice

¾ cup (125 g/4 oz) natural sultanas (golden raisins)

Makes 12 muffins

Pasta

When it comes to cereals and grains, there is plenty to choose from—rice, burghul wheat, buckwheat, pasta, noodles, couscous and polenta. Pasta dishes encourage the passing and sharing of Parmesan cheese and other topping delights. Delicious and comforting, they remind us of the conviviality of eating together. Even when eating alone, a simple pasta dish can be given a burst of new life with different topping ingredients.

For topping pasta, a good quality Parmesan or Romano cheese goes a long way when shaved — a nice change from grated (see page 89). And roasted nuts such as pine nuts, pecans or cashews add crunch and colour (see page 108 for how to roast nuts). Talking of colour, I often add quickly blanched broccoli florets and, always, fresh herbs. In summer, there's no going past fresh basil with its peppery fragrance and distinctive flavour. Whole fresh basil leaves scattered over pasta look beautiful and provide a burst of flavour when each one is consumed — a great freshener after a garlicky sauce. Here are a few tips for cooking pasta and for garnishing even the simplest of dishes to make it special.

Boiling Water for Pasta Quickly

Get started by putting your full electric jug or kettle on to boil. Then put 2–3 cups (500–700 mL/16–24 fl oz) cold water into the large pot you are going to cook your pasta in. Most importantly, put the lid on the pan and heat the water over the highest setting of your stove. When the jug boils, add the boiling water to the already bubbling water in the pasta pan. Then refill your jug or kettle and boil enough water until you have 4 litres (4 quarts/6½ imp pints) bubbling away in the pot.

Garnishes for Pasta Dishes

I'm sure we have all been served pasta topped with a sprig or two of parsley or some chopped parsley and, no doubt, with grated Parmesan cheese. These ingredients are fine, but be a bit more adventurous and try some of these tips occasionally. They don't take much time and yet provide a special touch that makes pasta dishes even more appealing than usual.

• • •

roasted pine nuts, walnuts, hazelnuts or almonds (see note on page 108 for how to roast nuts);

Roasted Capsicum (sweet pepper), peeled and cut into strips (page 16);

crumbled feta cheese or blue cheese;

sliced Blanched Broccoli (page 34);

halved cherry tomatoes and/or yellow teardrop tomatoes;

fresh basil leaves, whole or sliced with sharp kitchen scissors to prevent bruising;

fresh capsicum (sweet pepper) of various colours diced finely or cut into ultra-thin strips.

Fresh fettucine, now widely available at supermarkets and delicatessens, is a handy ingredient to pop into the refrigerator for a busy week. The fettucine in this delicious dish can be cooked with turmeric or saffron to provide a golden glow. Serve it hot as an entree or light meal, or cold as a salad, dressed simply with the juice of a lime or a lemon. And for either version, do try adding a handful of oven-roasted cashews for an interesting crunch.
(See Roasting Nuts and Seeds, page 108.)

Ingredients

500 g (1 lb) fresh fettucine

2 tablespoons olive oil

10 spring onions (scallions), sliced, green tops included

3–4 garlic cloves, crushed (pressed)

generous pinch of saffron or 1–1½ teaspoons turmeric powder

½ cup (125 mL/4 fl oz) vegetable stock

1 bunch spinach, trimmed and chopped

½ cup (90 g/3 oz) fresh Parmesan cheese, shaved or grated

cracked black pepper

Serves 4–6

Method

Begin by boiling the water (see note on page 85).

Once it is boiling rapidly, add the pasta and put the lid on the pan so that the water returns to the boil quickly.

Then remove the lid from the pan and cook the pasta at a rolling boil until it is al dente (tender, yet firm), about 5 minutes.

Meanwhile, heat 1 tablespoon of the oil in a frying pan (skillet) and stir-fry the spring onion, garlic and saffron (or turmeric) over a medium heat for 2 minutes.

Add the stock, then reduce the heat and cook gently for 2–3 minutes.

Meanwhile, heat the remaining oil in a large saucepan or wok and add the spinach.

Stir for a few seconds, then cover and cook until the spinach wilts down but still retains its rich green colour, about 3 minutes.

Drain the pasta well, then tip it into a large serving dish.

Pour the saffron (or turmeric) mixture over and toss quickly to ensure the pasta becomes coated with the mixture.

Spoon the spinach on top, then toss the pasta lightly to incorporate the spinach.

Scatter with shaved (see page 89) or grated Parmesan cheese, then dust with the pepper and serve at once.

A Note on Turmeric and Saffron

Turmeric provides a more intense golden colour and a definite spicy flavour to cooking, while saffron gives a creamy golden hue and a more subtle, yet distinctive taste. Turmeric is the choice of spice for everyday meals, due to the expense of saffron, the most expensive spice in the world. And no wonder, for saffron is the dried stamen of the crocus flower which must be picked by hand — and it takes 75,000 stamens to yield 500 g (1 lb) saffron!

Add More Pep with Pesto

Pesto, with its hearty and comforting flavour, is perfect for making a quick and cosy meal from whatever pasta you have in the cupboard. As soon as the pasta is ready, drain and tip into a serving dish. Then mix ¼ cup (60 mL/2 fl oz) of the hot pasta cooking water with 2–3 tablespoons of pesto sauce. Then quickly toss this mixture through the pasta.

Ingredients

8 Roma or other firm ripe tomatoes, cut into quarters or wedges

1 tablespoon extra virgin olive oil

4–6 garlic cloves, crushed (pressed)

1–2 teaspoons dried oregano

1–2 teaspoons dried sweet basil

½ teaspoon cracked black pepper

500 g (1 lb) pasta such as penne

½ cup (60 g/2 oz) grated or shaved Parmesan or Romano cheese

½ cup chopped parsley

3 tablespoons drained pitted (stoned) black (ripe) olives to garnish

2 tablespoons drained bottled capers to garnish

Serves 4

This is a lovely fragrant dish — and you don't have to wait until the cooking starts for the fragrance to emanate. Luckily, it is a quick dish, and once you start to prepare it, you and all those in the vicinity will be seduced by the delicious aromas of extra virgin olive oil, freshly crushed garlic, oregano and basil combined with the scent of fresh tomatoes. Of course, the intensity of the experience is really stepped up when the tomatoes start roasting in the oven. But the true beauty of assembling this dish lies in the fact that the time it takes to boil the water and cook the pasta is the same as the time it takes to roast the tomatoes — so they can both be happening at once.

Method

Preheat the oven to 180°C/350°F.

Place the tomatoes in a large bowl.

Combine the oil with the garlic and drizzle over the tomatoes.

Sprinkle the oregano, basil and black pepper over, then toss the mixture well to ensure that the tomatoes are coated with the flavoured oil.

Arrange the tomatoes in a baking dish which has been brushed with oil.

Shaved Cheese

This sounds as if the cheese has sprouted whiskers, but all it means is shaving off thin slivers of cheese using a vegetable peeler. This works best with particularly firm cheese like Parmesan and Romano.

Bake for 20 minutes.

Meanwhile, set a large pan of water to boil for the pasta (see note on page 85).

Once the water is boiling rapidly, add the pasta and cook until it is al dente (tender, yet firm), about 12–15 minutes.

Drain the pasta and tip it into a large serving dish.

Add the roasted tomatoes complete with the juices, then toss the pasta to coat it with the tomatoes.

Sprinkle the Parmesan (or Romano) cheese and parsley over and toss lightly.

Serve at once scattered with the olives and capers.

Add a Touch of Blue

If you are a fan of blue cheeses, try crumbling a little over pasta just before you serve it, in place of the Parmesan cheese.

Even though it's really quick and easy, this dish is beautiful to serve for a special meal. It can be served cold as a salad.

Method

500 g (1 lb) pasta such as penne, shells or bows

500 g (1 lb) broccoli

1 tablespoon olive oil

6 spring onions (scallions), sliced, green tops included

125 g (4 oz) walnuts, chopped roughly

2–3 garlic cloves, crushed (pressed)

cracked black pepper

½ cup chopped Italian flat-leafed parsley

½ cup (90 g/ 3 oz) grated Parmesan cheese

1 lemon, cut into wedges

Serves 4–6

Begin by boiling the water (see note on page 85).

Once it is boiling rapidly, add the pasta and put the lid on the pan so that the water returns to the boil quickly.

Remove the lid from the pan and cook the pasta at a rolling boil until it is al dente (tender, yet firm), about 12 minutes.

Meanwhile, cut the broccoli into florets. Then trim the coarse end from the stalks and cut them into thin sticks, or slice them in half lengthways, then crossways.

If you have a microwave oven, place the stalks and the florets in a microwave-proof dish with a lid and cook on high for 2 minutes.

Remove from the hot dish at once to prevent further cooking.

If you don't have a microwave, steam the florets and stalks together in a steamer insert over 1 cup (250 mL/8 fl oz) boiling water for 5 minutes only.

Heat the oil in a frying pan (skillet) and stir-fry the spring onion and walnuts over a medium heat for 2 minutes.

Add the garlic and continue stir-frying for 2 minutes.

Drain the pasta well, then tip it into a large serving dish.

Top with the broccoli, then the walnut mixture, then dust with the pepper and sprinkle with the parsley.

Serve at once with the Parmesan cheese and lemon wedges.

This is a very quick and easy sauce to whip up when the hunger pangs hit. It takes as long to cook as it takes to bring a large pan of water to the boil and cook the pasta — very convenient!

Method

Heat the oil over a medium heat.

Stir in the onion, cover the pan and cook for 5 minutes. This will help cook the onion thoroughly and quickly in a minimum of oil without burning. Even so, take care to peep into the pan once or twice to make sure the onion is not catching on the bottom of the pan. It also helps to give the pan a quick stir or shake to prevent the onion from sticking.

Add the garlic, spring onion, oregano and basil and stir for a minute before cooking as before with the lid on the pan, for 2 minutes.

Stir in the tomato and tomato paste and bring to the boil, stirring. Reduce the heat to medium-low and cook, covered, for about 20 minutes.

Stir in the wine (or apple juice) and cook, uncovered, over a medium-high heat for 5 minutes.

Season to taste with freshly ground or cracked black pepper.

Bottled Pasta Sauce at Your Service

Always have several bottles of a good brand of prepared pasta sauce lying in wait in your pantry. Pasta sauce is really handy to add flavour to soups, to top pizzas with or to add to canned (tinned) or cooked beans with a few drops of Tabasco Sauce for quickly made Chilli Beans (page 131). It can even be blended until smooth in a food processor or blender with a slurp of hot chilli sauce to make a great last-minute sauce for topping nachos or tacos.

Ingredients

2–3 teaspoons olive oil

1 medium-large onion, diced or chopped finely, about 1½ cups (225 g/8 oz)

2–3 garlic cloves, crushed (pressed)

4 spring onions (scallions), sliced, green tops included

1 teaspoon dried oregano

1 teaspoon dried sweet basil

810 g (1 large can (tin)/1¾ lb) crushed tomatoes

1–2 tablespoons tomato paste (purée)

3 tablespoons white wine *or* apple juice

cracked black pepper

Serves 4–6

Pesto Sauce

It's easy to become passionate about pesto. The passion is all to do with the intoxicating aroma and taste of fresh basil married to the full-bodied flavour of garlic. And as if this wasn't enough, roasted pine nuts and grated Parmesan can be thrown in for good measure. With the grinding of a peppermill and perhaps a pinch of salt, you're home and hosed! Even though it seems Pesto Sauce contains a considerable amount of fat from the olive oil, pine nuts and Parmesan, remember, pesto is a potent sauce and need only be used in small amounts. When using it to serve with freshly cooked pasta, you should also dilute the sauce with ¼ cup (60 mL/2 fl oz) of the pasta water, so remember this before you triumphantly strain your cooked pasta into a colander or strainer perched over your sink!

In this book you will see that I use Pesto Sauce in a variety of dishes from soups to spreads. It's perfect for adding a mere spoonful to a bubbling pot of soup just before serving. And it's a wonderful standby for those times when you crave pasta but don't have the time to cook a tomato sauce. So, as soon as you have a good supply of fresh basil, make up a good-sized jar of Pesto Sauce, for it will keep for some weeks in the refrigerator. If not for any other reason, enjoy the summer months for the bounty of fresh basil that is available. In cooler months, I survive by having a jar or two of a good brand of commercially prepared pesto on standby in my pantry.

Method

Ingredients

3 cups fresh basil leaves

1 cup fresh parsley sprigs

4 garlic cloves, crushed (pressed)

4 tablespoons olive oil

3 tablespoons roasted pine nuts

2–3 tablespoons grated Parmesan cheese (optional)

pepper

Makes about 2 cups (500 mL/16 fl oz)

Using a food processor or a sharp knife, chop the basil and parsley, then add the garlic and oil.

Process for 20 seconds or so, then add the pine nuts and, if using, the Parmesan cheese.

Serve at once, or place the pesto in a screw-top jar in the refrigerator until ready to use.

Other Nuts, Other Herbs

Pine nuts are really lovely in Pesto Sauce, especially when their flavour is coaxed out by the roasting process. However, they can be a little pricey, so you may want to use other nuts for a change, like cashew nuts or even hazelnuts, which contribute a more intense nutty flavour to pesto. I love pesto for the basil which gives it its character, so I would not totally replace it with another herb, but I often substitute some of the amount with parsley (the Italian flat-leaf variety is my favourite) or beautiful rocket (arugula) lettuce for variety.

Extra Virgin Olive Oil

I like using extra virgin olive oil for salad dishes where the effect I am seeking is one of robust and alluring flavour. This is especially obvious in Rich and Red Bean Salad (page 132) and Salad of White Beans (page 136) which are greatly enhanced by the burst of flavour only extra virgin olive oil can provide.

Wonton skins are the magic ingredient here — they are very convenient to have hanging around in your refrigerator because they greatly reduce the usual cooking time for lasagne. They are also extremely quick and easy to use. Like pasta, wonton skins are made from flour, water and a little salt, sometimes with the addition of egg. The dough is kneaded and rolled out into thin sheets of 'pastry', then cut into characteristically round or square shapes, packaged and chilled. Wonton skins can be found in the refrigerated section of Asian grocery stores.

As for most lasagne recipes, this one is best served the next day after cooking when the flavours have truly mingled and the texture has become firmer, making it easier to slice and serve. But for hungry people who want to eat now, this is a great dish to assemble in individual ramekins. In fact, you can even buy round wonton skins which seem to be especially designed for this purpose because they fit standard round ramekins perfectly.

Fresh Basil

Who can resist the distinctive sweet peppery fragrance of fresh basil? To me, it is one of the most beautiful flavours of summer. Enjoy using it to make ever-popular Pesto Sauce (page 92), or use tiny leaves to garnish finger foods and canapes, or to toss into salads. Use kitchen scissors to shred basil leaves without bruising them and scatter over hot dishes just before serving. Larger whole basil leaves are also fabulous as wrappings for bite-sized morsels of food such as feta cheese: spear the little package with a toothpick and decorate with half a tiny cherry tomato or yellow teardrop tomato.

Method

Preheat the oven to 190°C/375°F.

Heat the oil in a frying pan (skillet) or large saucepan with a lid, then add the prepared spinach.

Stir briefly, then cook over a medium heat with the lid on the pan, until the spinach has wilted but is still a vibrant green colour.

Use one third of the Pasta Sauce to make a layer on the bottom of a lasagne dish that has been brushed with a little olive oil.

Top with a layer of wonton skins, then follow with layers of vegetables and sauce as follows, with wonton skins in-between — half the Garlic Mushrooms, half the roasted capsicum, all the spinach, one third of the Pasta Sauce; then the rest of the Garlic Mushrooms, the rest of the roasted capsicum and, lastly, the remaining Pasta Sauce.

Sprinkle the mozzarella over, then the Parmesan.

Bake in a moderately hot oven for about 30 minutes.

Allow to stand for 5–10 minutes before slicing and serving topped with whole fresh basil leaves.

Ingredients

2 teaspoons olive oil

1 bunch spinach, washed well, dried and shredded

1 quantity Quick and Tasty Pasta Sauce (page 91)

1 packet (250 g/ 8 oz) wonton skins

1 quantity Garlic Mushrooms (page 29)

2–3 red capsicums (sweet peppers), roasted and peeled (page 16)

1 cup (125 g/4 oz) grated mozzarella cheese

1 tablespoon grated Parmesan cheese

fresh basil leaves for garnishing

Serves 6–8

95

Noodles

When people say, 'Use your noodle,' I know just what they mean. I agree, for these days an amazing variety of noodles is available to us. It's worth while exploring Asian grocery stores for an educational experience in terms of all the wonderful ingredients available, but especially for the many kinds of noodles. Fresh and dried varieties can be purchased as required or stored for later use. Nutritious, economical and quickly prepared, they certainly add change and interest to the menu. Try the wholegrain varieties and those made from eggs, mung bean starch (see the note on Cellophane Noodles opposite) and rice (Rice Vermicelli, opposite). The beauty of noodles, as with many of my favourite ingredients, is that they are so versatile and allow plenty of scope when it comes to providing a backdrop for a host of dishes from rich peanut (groundnut) and coconut-infused concoctions to those with a blast of chilli to get us kick-started.

Have you Tried Rice Vermicelli?

These only need 10 minutes' soaking in hot water before tossing with some quickly cooked vegetables and a drizzling of a tasty sauce such as Garlic and Ginger Sauce (page 51); also wonderful drizzled with Sweet Chilli Sauce (page 53) and scattered with roasted peanuts (groundnuts) and chopped coriander (cilantro).

Or Cellophane Noodles?

As their name implies, cellophane noodles become transparent when cooked. They are made from mung bean starch rather than wheat flour. Like pasta, they can take from only a few minutes to up to 20 minutes to cook, depending upon their thickness. Great served topped or tossed with stir-fries or spicy curries.

New Ways with Noodles

Here are a few ways to get you started with dressing up your favourite cooked noodles, rather than relying on the little foil packages that accompany instant noodle concoctions:

◆ stir-fried ultra-thin strips of capsicum (sweet pepper), spring onions (scallions) and carrots (these can be cooking while you cook your noodles as they take the same time);

◆ Blanched Broccoli (page 34) and a drizzling of Garlic and Ginger Sauce (page 51);

◆ finely shredded Chinese greens tossed through the steaming hot noodles, then drizzled with Sweet Chilli Sauce (page 53);

◆ strips or cubes of tofu sprinkled with soy sauce and tossed with thin sticks of pickled vegetables such as Quick Pickled Carrots (page 32) and pickled daikon radish (see note on page 49).

Ingredients

2–3 teaspoons sesame oil

1 onion, sliced into thin half rings

2 medium carrots, scrubbed or peeled and cut into thin sticks

2 stalks broccoli, cut into small florets, stalks sliced thinly

2–3 teaspoons grated ginger

1 teaspoon finely sliced, seeded chillies (chilli peppers) or 1 teaspoon chilli powder

4–6 garlic cloves, crushed (pressed)

2 cabbage leaves, shredded

500 g (1 lb) fresh hokkien noodles

250 g (8 oz) firm tofu, cut into ½-cm thick sticks or 1-cm cubes

1 cup (250 mL/ 8 fl oz) vegetable stock

2–3 tablespoons soy sauce

2 tablespoons mirin or 4 tablespoons apple juice

60 g (2 oz) piece pickled daikon radish, cut into thin strips

Serves 4–6

There seem to be quite a number of flavouring ingredients in this dish. They are all necessary, however, to produce the wonderful blend of flavours so much loved in Asian cooking. I'm talking about grated fresh ginger, crushed garlic, sliced chillies (chilli peppers), soy sauce, mirin and aromatic sesame oil — mmm, these will have your tastebuds warming up while the dish is cooking!

Method

Heat the oil in a wok or large saucepan, then add the onions and stir-fry for 1 minute.

Stir in the carrots, then place a lid on the pan and cook over a medium heat for 5 minutes.

Stir in the broccoli stalks, ginger, chilli and garlic, then cover and cook for 5 minutes more.

Stir in the broccoli florets and cabbage, then cover and cook for 10 minutes.

Then stir in the noodles and tofu, taking care not to break up the tofu, and cover and heat through for 1 minute.

Meanwhile, combine the stock, soy sauce and mirin (or apple juice) and add the mixture to the pan.

Cover and cook for 1 minute.

Remove from the heat and toss the daikon radish strips through.

Transfer the noodles to a large serving dish if you have one, or serve directly into individual bowls.

Mirin

A popular sweet Japanese cooking wine made from rice, mirin is superb added to tender crisp vegetable dishes, cooked beans and dipping sauces. Good-quality mirin has a sweet flavour produced during the fermentation process rather than added in the form of barley malt or glucose. It is available from Asian grocery stores and health food stores.

Hokkien Noodles

These golden-yellow or creamy coloured noodles are available fresh or dried from Asian grocery stores, and sometimes from supermarkets. I like the fresh variety, not only because it only requires a few minutes' cooking, but also because the noodles develop a wonderful tender texture without losing their shape. Have some on standby in your refrigerator where they can be kept for up to 1 week. They can be frozen too, so next time you're in an Asian grocery store, pick up a few extra bags of these fabulous noodles.

This soup sounds suspiciously like a cure for hangovers! And in fact, I do like to use it to nurture loved ones who are feeling a little off-colour as it is tasty and comforting. This type of soup, along with Golden Pumpkin Soup (page 28), is my vegetarian answer to the traditional cup of chicken soup for the ailing.

Method

Ingredients

2 teaspoons sesame oil

1 onion, cut into thin half rings

2 carrots, scrubbed or peeled and cut into thin slices or half moons

1 bunch spring onions (scallions), trimmed and sliced, green tops included

3–4 garlic cloves, crushed (pressed)

1 teaspoon finely sliced seeded chillies (chilli peppers) (optional)

6 cups (1.5 litres/ 2½ imp pints) vegetable stock

250 g (8 oz) soba noodles

250 g (8 oz) beanshoots

125 g (4 oz) snow peas (mangetout), trimmed

soy sauce

Serves 4

Heat the oil in a large saucepan and stir-fry the onion over a medium heat for 1 minute. Cover and cook for 2 minutes.

Then stir in the carrot and cover and cook for 5 minutes, stirring now and then.

Add the spring onion, garlic and, if using, the chillies and stir-fry the mixture for 2 minutes.

Add the stock and stir well.

Cover and bring the mixture to the boil, then add the noodles. Cook for 5 minutes or so, or until the noodles are cooked (they should be tender, yet firm).

Immediately stir in the beanshoots and snow peas, and cover and cook for 1 minute only to prevent overcooking the noodles.

Season to taste with the soy sauce and serve at once.

Soba Noodles

Soba noodles are made from buckwheat flour or a mixture of wholewheat flour and buckwheat flour. Pasta varieties like these noodles are more nutritious than those prepared from white flour, containing more than twice as much dietary fibre and more vitamins and minerals. They have a characteristic flavour, but, more importantly, a firm texture which ensures that they hold their shape when cooked. Soba noodles are much valued in Japan for this chewy, yet tender texture which is attributed to the care taken during manufacture, especially with the drying process.

Rice

Rice is a life-saver when it comes to simple, nourishing meals. After all, it has been the staple food and a real life-saver for millions of people for centuries. I usually have a container of Cooked Brown Rice (see page 102) in the refrigerator at some time during the week, which I can whip up into a tasty salad or side dish, or use as the base for stuffing vegetables like capsicum (sweet pepper) or eggplant (aubergine). It's also great for adding to cooked vegetable mixtures along with grated tasty (mature cheddar) cheese for vegetable slices and pies. Be adventurous and try the many other varieties of rice — from fragrant jasmine rice to sticky glutinous rice — so readily available to us these days.

Brown rice contains more dietary fibre, vitamins and minerals than white rice and has a satisfying chewy texture. Cooked brown rice is perfect for making stir-fried dishes because the grains are far less likely to stick together. I prefer to cook it by the absorption method outlined below rather than boiling it in masses of water because this retains the flavour and superior texture of the rice.

Method

Ingredients

3 cups (600 g/ 21 oz) brown rice

6 cups (1.5 litres/ 2½ imp pints) water

pinch of salt (optional)

Makes about 4 cups

Place the rice in a sieve and wash it in one or two rinses of water.

Drain well and put the rice with the 3 cups of water and, if using, the salt, into a saucepan.

Cover and bring the rice to the boil, then reduce the heat and cook the rice gently for 25 minutes.

Turn off the heat and allow the rice to stand, covered, for another 5–10 minutes.

Fluff up the rice with a fork and serve.

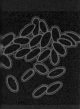

Quick Cook Brown Rice

For speed, try using the quick cook variety of brown rice. For those who prefer the softer texture of white rice, Quick Cook Brown Rice has a similar texture but is more nutritious.

Method

Place the rice in a sieve and wash it in one or two rinses of water.

Drain well and put the rice with the 3½ cups of water and, if using, the salt, into a saucepan.

Cover and bring the rice to the boil, then reduce the heat and cook the rice over a very gentle heat for 15 minutes.

Turn off the heat and allow the rice to stand, covered, for another 5–10 minutes.

Fluff up the rice with a fork and serve.

Ingredients

3 cups (600 g/ 21 oz) short grain white rice

4½ cups (1.05 litres/ 2 imp pints) water

pinch of salt (optional)

Makes about 6 cups

Shortgrain or Longgrain?

Use shortgrain rice when you wish to achieve a softer, 'stickier'-textured rice which is especially suitable for recipes such as Sushi Rice (see next page). Or try using glutinous rice — a form of shortgrain rice which develops a sticky texture when cooked. Use longgrain rice for dishes which require the rice to retain separate grains, such as fried rice.

Pickled Ginger

This is superb as a filling ingredient for sushi rolls, for garnishing Japanese-style dishes and for adding a sit-up-and-take-notice flavour to pita bread or Mountain Bread Roll-ups (page 76). It is available at Asian grocery stores.

103

The characteristic sharp edge of sushi rice is provided by a vinegar mixture which is poured over and stirred through the rice as soon as it is cooked. Choose a quality white wine vinegar rather than regular white vinegar for this task, otherwise the flavour will be too strong. I like to use half brown rice vinegar (available at Asian grocery stores) which has a slightly sharp edge to it, but an overall mellow flavour, and half white wine vinegar. Mirin, a type of Japanese cooking wine (see note on page 99), adds a sweet light note to counteract the sharpness of the vinegar. Many people like to add a tablespoon of sugar to the vinegar mixture, but I settle for 1–2 teaspoons which do nicely when mirin is used.

Method

Ingredients

2 tablespoons mirin or dry sherry

3 tablespoons white wine vinegar

2 teaspoons sugar

pinch of salt

1 quantity freshly cooked shortgrain White Rice (page 103)

Makes about 6 cups

Place the mirin (or sherry), vinegar, sugar and salt into a small saucepan and bring the mixture to the boil, stirring to dissolve the sugar.

Reduce the heat and cook gently for 1 minute, then pour over the rice and mix well.

Note on Nori

Nori is dried laver, which is a type of seaweed. It is pressed into thin sheets and then dried and is one of the most popular sea vegetables because of its pleasant texture and attractive appearance. You're most likely to see it used for wrapping sushi; however it is also delicious toasted and crumbled over soups and salads or cut into thin strips and used as a garnish for grain, noodle and vegetable dishes. To toast nori, simply wave it over a gas flame for a few seconds until the colour changes from a very dark green to a lighter olive shade. In the toasting process the flavour develops beautifully. Both plain and toasted nori is available from Asian grocery stores and health food stores.

This is for you, Neil. These wonderful sushi rolls with a difference wear their rice on the outside, dressed only with a film of roasted sesame seeds. For toasting nori, see note on opposite page and for toasting seeds, the note on page 108.

Method

Combine the carrot, spring onion and pickled vegetables.

Lay the nori sheets out flat and cover with the Sushi Rice, pressing the rice down so that it adheres to the nori.

Turn the nori over and spread the vegetable mixture evenly over the other side.

Roll up the nori carefully and firmly to form a cylindrical roll. Spread the sesame seeds evenly over a generous length of kitchen or baking paper, then run each of the rolls over the seeds, pressing the rolls firmly against the seeds so that they stick to the rice.

Using a sharp knife, cut each of the rolls into 6 neat pieces.

Ingredients

1 carrot, scrubbed and grated coarsely

3 spring onions (scallions), finely sliced, green tops included

4 tablespoons chopped pickled vegetables (see note below)

4 sheets toasted nori

1 quantity Sushi Rice (page 104)

½ cup (80 g/3 oz) toasted sesame seeds

Makes 24

Have You Tried Pickled Vegetables?

Pickled ginger, daikon radish and other pickled vegetables are available in jars or vacuum packs from Asian grocery stores. Used in small amounts, they make tasty and colourful fillings or toppings for sandwiches, nori rolls or canapés.

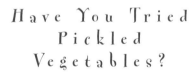

I just love colour, and these are a sight for sore eyes! In fact, sunglasses are a must if you are not used to the brilliant hue of Pickled Red Cabbage Leaves or pickled daikon radish (see note on page 49)! Usually it's best to do very little to vegetables other than to serve them fresh or lightly cooked. Here, the pickling process brings out the rich hue just waiting to be released in red cabbage, rather similar to the way that blanching brings out the vivid green of broccoli.

I use Pickled Red Cabbage Leaves to wrap up the rice in Psychedelic Sushi Rolls (see recipe opposite). For this, you'll need whole leaves, but don't worry if you have a rather tricky red cabbage that doesn't let go of its leaves when you're trying to separate them. If some do tear, they can simply be overlapped when assembling the rolls.

Method

Ingredients

6 red cabbage leaves, coarse spines removed

1 cup (250 mL/ 8 fl oz) apple juice

3 cups (750 mL/ 24 fl oz) white vinegar

1 teaspoon black peppercorns

½ cup (125 g/ 4 oz) sugar

½ teaspoon salt

Makes 6

'Refresh' the cabbage leaves by dunking in or splashing them with cold water and shake dry.

Place the apple juice, vinegar, peppercorns, sugar and salt in a large saucepan and bring the mixture to the boil.

One by one, immerse the cabbage leaves and boil each for 2 minutes, then remove with tongs and place on a large plate or platter to cool.

Use as required, or place in a covered container and refrigerate for up to 4 days.

Keep the pickling liquid to use for Quick Pickled Carrots (page 32).

Even if you choose to wrap the rice in nori rather than pickled red cabbage leaves, the Red Cabbage Pickle (page 45) or Ruby Red Salad (page 44) in this recipe are simply bursting with colour. See the note on toasting nori on page 104.

Method

Combine the carrot, spring onion and pickle.

Lay 4 of the cabbage leaves (or the 4 nori sheets) out flat. Use pieces of the remaining 2 leaves to cover any splits or cracks in the flat cabbage leaves.

Cover the cabbage leaves (or nori sheets) evenly with the Sushi Rice, except for a 2-cm (1-in) strip across the edge furthest from you.

Arrange the vegetable mixture in a strip across the centre of the rice, then arrange the sticks of daikon radish and whole snow peas evenly alongside.

Applying firm, even pressure, roll the cabbage leaves (or nori sheets) up to form 4 neat rolls.

Using a sharp knife, cut each of the rolls into 6 pieces.

Ingredients

2 small-medium carrots, scrubbed or peeled and cut into thin matchsticks

4 spring onions (scallions), finely sliced, green tops included

4 tablespoons Red Cabbage Pickle (page 45) or Ruby Red Salad (page 44)

6 Pickled Red Cabbage Leaves (opposite page) or 4 sheets toasted nori (page 104)

1 quantity Sushi Rice (page 104)

½ cup pickled daikon radish, cut into thin sticks

12 snow peas (mangetout), trimmed and blanched

Makes 24

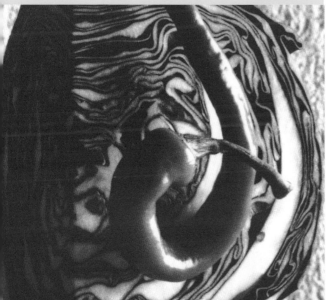

This rice has a lovely roasted nutty flavour imparted by the sesame oil and the roasted cashews. Serve with stir-fried vegetables or hot spicy dishes. Or use as a filling for Scrumptious Lettuce Rolls (page 110).

Method

Ingredients

2 teaspoons sesame oil

1 cup (150 g/5 oz) cashew nuts

4 spring onions (scallions), sliced finely, green tops included

4 cups Cooked Brown Rice (page 102), chilled

2 tablespoons soy sauce

pepper

Serves 4

Heat the oil in a wok or frying pan (skillet) and stir-fry the cashews and spring onion over a medium-high heat until the nuts become a light golden-brown colour.

Add the rice and stir over the heat for 2 minutes, then cover and cook over a medium heat for 5 minutes.

Sprinkle the soy sauce over, then mix through with pepper to taste.

Serve hot or cold.

Roasting Nuts and Seeds

Roasting brings out the sweet flavour of nuts and seeds, and it can be done without any added fat or oil. This can be done in the oven or on top of the stove. In the oven, simply spread the nuts or seeds out on a baking tray (sheet) and bake at 200°C/400°CF for about 20 minutes. For the stove method, heat a heavy based frying pan (skillet) over a medium heat for 5 minutes or so, stirring the nuts and seeds as they roast to prevent them from burning.

There's something about the aroma of roasting sesame seeds that attracts people to the kitchen. Serve this rice with stir-fried or braised vegetables. I enjoy teaming it up with Garlic Mushrooms (page 29) for a really tasty dish.

Method

Heat the oil in a wok or frying pan (skillet) and stir-fry the onion for 1 minute, then cover and cook for 5 minutes.

Add the chives (or spring onion), mustard seeds and sesame seeds and stir-fry over a medium-high heat until the sesame seeds become a light golden-brown colour.

Add the rice and stir over the heat for 2 minutes, then cover and cook over a medium heat for 5 minutes.

Sprinkle the soy sauce over, then mix through with pepper to taste.

Serve hot or cold garnished with parsley (or coriander).

Ingredients

2 teaspoons sesame oil

1 onion, finely diced, about 1 cup (150 g/5 oz)

3 tablespoons finely sliced chives or spring onions (scallions), green tops included

1 teaspoon yellow mustard seeds

2 tablespoons sesame seeds

4 cups Cooked Brown Rice (page 102)

1 tablespoon soy sauce

cracked black pepper

½ cup chopped parsley or coriander (cilantro)

Serves 4

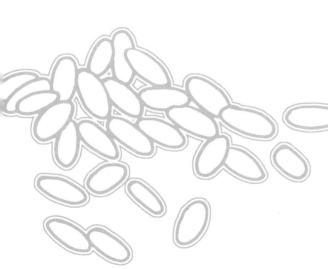

Scrumptious Lettuce Rolls

Ideal for a quickly assembled meal if you have Cashew or Sesame Rice (pages 108 or 109) to hand. Enjoy these rolls as a quick snack or as a starter with a bowl of Sweet Chilli Sauce (page 53). Try using lettuce leaves of varying colours to produce a dramatic effect when serving.

Method

Ingredients

8 large lettuce leaves, trimmed

1 quantity Quick Cashew Rice (page 108) or Roasted Sesame Rice (page 109)

Makes 8

Place ½ cup of the rice at one end of each lettuce leaf, then, applying firm, even pressure, fold the sides of the lettuce over the filling and roll up firmly to form a neat package, ensuring that the edges of the lettuce leaves are tucked underneath.

Serve at once.

A tasty vegetable and brown rice dish enriched with melted cheese or roasted nuts and topped with crisp pastry. This recipe is designed to yield a large number of servings so that left-overs can be reheated for delicious impromptu meals. For keeping longer than 2 or 3 days, freeze single or family serve portions of the slice for thawing and reheating later.

Method

Preheat the oven to 190°C/375°F.

Heat the oil in a wok or large saucepan.

Add the onion and stir briefly over a medium heat. Cover and cook for 5 minutes to soften the onion quickly.

Add the garlic, carrot and celery and stir over the heat for 1 minute. Cover and cook for 5 minutes.

Then stir the tomato and parsley through.

Remove from the heat and stir in the rice and cheese (or cashews or pine nuts) and season to taste with the soy sauce and pepper.

Arrange two sheets of the filo pastry on the base of a baking dish that has been brushed with a little of the additional oil.

Spread some of the vegetable mixture out in an even layer over the pastry.

Layer the remaining 10 filo sheets, with the rest of the vegetable mixture, arranging 2 sheets at a time.

Using a pastry brush, brush a little yoghurt over each double layer of pastry, except for the very top layer.

Then, using a clean pastry brush, brush the top with the remaining oil and, if using, sprinkle with sesame seeds.

Bake in a moderately hot oven for 20 minutes, or until the pastry is a golden-brown colour.

Ingredients

2–3 teaspoons oil

2 large onions, diced, about 3 cups (450 g/1 lb)

6 garlic cloves, crushed (pressed)

4 carrots, scrubbed and diced

4 celery sticks, trimmed and diced

3 tomatoes, diced or chopped or 425 g (15 oz) canned (tinned) crushed tomatoes

1 cup chopped parsley

4 cups Cooked Brown Rice (page 102)

1 cup (125 g/4 oz) grated tasty (mature cheddar) cheese or ½ cup (90 g/3 oz) roasted cashew nuts or pine nuts

1–2 tablespoons soy sauce

pepper

additional 2 teaspoons oil

12 sheets filo (phyllo) pastry

3 tablespoons yoghurt

1–2 tablespoons sesame seeds (optional)

Serves 8

Buckwheat Pilaf

What makes this dish distinctive are the robust flavours of buckwheat and mushrooms. It is a great autumn or winter dish when flavoursome field mushrooms can be found.
(See notes on blanching broccoli florets on page 34 and on roasting nuts on page 108.)

Ingredients

3 teaspoons peanut (groundnut) or sesame oil

2 large onions, diced or chopped finely, about 3 cups (450 g/1 lb)

2 cups (360 g/12 oz) buckwheat

1 cup (125 g/4 oz) mushrooms, trimmed and sliced

2½ cups (625 mL/20 fl oz) vegetable stock

½ cup chopped coriander (cilantro)

1 teaspoon honey

2 tablespoons soy sauce

2 cups (115 g/4 oz) broccoli florets, blanched

⅓ cup (2 oz) pine nuts, roasted

Serves 4

Method

Heat the oil in a wok or large frying pan (skillet) and stir the onion over a medium heat for 1 minute, then cover and cook for 5 minutes to soften the onion quickly.

Add the buckwheat and stir over the heat for 2–3 minutes to impart a roasted flavour.

Add the mushrooms and the stock, reduce the heat and cook gently for 20 minutes.

Add the coriander, honey and soy sauce and continue to cook gently for 5 minutes more.

Add the broccoli florets and cover and cook for 2 minutes to heat them through.

Serve scattered with the roasted pine nuts.

Polenta Potential

Polenta has long been enjoyed by the people of northern Italy. Made from ground dried corn, polenta is also known as cornmeal. Polenta is the cheerful golden colour of corn, and is traditionally prepared rather like a thick porridge. It can be used as an accompaniment in place of mashed potatoes, or served with a pasta sauce. It is really worth while preparing a tray of polenta in advance so that quick meals such as Grilled Polenta (page 115) with its crisp golden surface can be whipped up at just a few minutes' notice.

In the time it takes to cook a batch of the fine-ground quick polenta available these days, do give a thought to the cooks who still cook polenta in the traditional manner. This involves using a thick, coarse-grained polenta, which takes much longer to cook. These people endure almost an hour of constantly stirring a mixture that bubbles and spits like a hot mud pool. It's no wonder that polenta cooks wised up to the fact that it was necessary to dress accordingly — that is, to wear a garment with long sleeves to protect the tender skin on the undersides of the wrists from the intermittent spitting of hot polenta. This is a tip I advise even for the modern cook who need only stir the mixture for 10 minutes or so. Another trick to protect yourself from the onslaught of the luscious golden goo is to make sure you use a wooden spoon with a very long handle when stirring the pot!

Method

Ingredients

**4 cups (1 litre/
1¾ imp pints)
vegetable stock**

**1 cup (175 g/6 oz)
fine polenta
(cornmeal)**

pepper

Serves 6

Bring the stock to the boil in a medium-large saucepan and gradually add the polenta, stirring constantly.

Reduce the heat and, still stirring constantly, cook the polenta until it reaches a consistency similar to thin mashed potatoes, about 10 minutes.

Season to taste with the pepper and serve at once, or place in a lightly oiled cake tin (pan) and allow to cool and set.

Polenta

Polenta is an extremely versatile food which can be served as a mash, rather like mashed potatoes, or poured into a prepared cake tin (pan), flan tin or terrine dish and set aside until it cools and becomes firm. Once firm, it can be cut into cubes and served tossed with pasta sauce, much as you would serve gnocchi. Or it can be cut into neat slices or wedges and grilled (broiled) until golden-brown (see Grilled Polenta on page 115 (opposite).

All it takes to prepare this quick nutritious dish is a roaring hot grill (broiler) to brown the slices of polenta under. When Basic Polenta (page 114, opposite) sets firm, it can be sliced and grilled until golden-brown; it makes a quick satisfying meal when served with a crisp salad and a vegetable side dish such as Braised Capsicum (page 20) which can be whipped up while you heat the grill and brown the polenta.

Method

Cut the polenta into desired shapes such as wedges, rectangles or squares, or use Polenta Shapes (see below).

When the grill (broiler) is hot, cook the polenta until it becomes an appetising golden-brown on both sides.

Serve hot or warm.

Ingredients

1 quantity Basic Polenta (page 114, opposite), set until firm

Serves 6

Quick Polenta Shapes

Fine polenta takes only 10 minutes to prepare, and if you wish to serve it quickly in a neat shape rather than straight on to plates as a thick golden mash, then invest in some small moulds. Chill these and you will have your heart-shapes or tartlets of polenta in 10–15 minutes or so. If using special moulds doesn't tickle your fancy, you can simply pop the prepared polenta into oiled muffin tins (pans) instead. About 18 polenta shapes can be made from the Basic Polenta recipe when using muffin tins (pans) or small moulds.

Making polenta into shapes is convenient because small shapes will cool more quickly than a whole pan of polenta. And during the 10–15 minutes the polenta takes to cool, you can whip up a sauce which will bring a blaze of colour to the polenta, such as those mentioned on page 116.

When the polenta shapes are really firm, place them under a hot grill (broiler) until they turn a light golden-brown. Serve at once, or at room temperature.

Serve Quick Polenta Shapes with fresh crusty bread and steamed vegetables. My first preference would be steamed broccoli which can also be prepared in a flash in the microwave (page 34). Or why not go for green beans or asparagus when in season.

Serve with a tasty sauce such as Scarlet Sauce (page 17), Quick & Tasty Pasta Sauce (page 91) or a vegetable dish such as Vegetable Streamers (page 19) or Braised Capsicum (Sweet Pepper) (page 20). Make plenty of this as it is great revisited — sliced and grilled (broiled) until golden-brown.

Method

Ingredients

4 cups (1 litre/ 1¾ imp pints) vegetable stock

1 onion, diced or chopped, about 1 cup (150 g/5 oz)

2 garlic cloves, crushed (pressed)

1 stick celery, diced

1 large carrot, scrubbed and diced

½ red capsicum (sweet pepper), diced, about ¾ cup (150 g/ 5 oz)

1 cup (175 g/6 oz) sweet corn kernels

1 cup (175 g/6 oz) polenta

½ cup (60 g/2 oz) grated tasty (mature cheddar) cheese and additional ½ cup grated tasty cheese

¼ teaspoon cracked black pepper

½ cup chopped parsley

Serves 6–8

Preheat the oven to 200°C/400°F.

Bring the stock to the boil in a large saucepan and add the onion, garlic, celery, carrot, capsicum and corn kernels.

Return the mixture to the boil and slowly add a 'stream' of polenta, stirring constantly.

Cook, stirring, for 5–10 minutes until the mixture resembles creamy mashed potatoes.

Add the cheese, pepper and parsley and spread out in a prepared 23-cm (9-in) flan tin.

Set aside to cool, then put in the freezer for 10 minutes to allow the mixture to become quite firm.

After 10 minutes, take the tin out of the freezer and sprinkle the additional cheese over the top of the polenta.

Bake for 10 minutes, or until the top is golden-brown.

Cooking in Cast Iron

There is something to be said for purchasing a cast-iron frying pan (skillet) with a cast-iron handle so that it can be used in the oven. Even if you only use it to bake corn bread in the oven, rest assured it can also be put to good use for roasting spices, nuts and seeds on top of the stove and for cooking an endless array of dishes.

This corn bread was inspired by my newfound friend, author Crescent Dragonwagon (see page 57). If you have already become familiar with my passion for colour, I know you'll understand my attraction to the golden hue of polenta. To be able to whip up such a quick and homely dish, all you need are the basic ingredients and 30 minutes or so up your sleeve. I usually make corn bread on those cold blustery days that Melbourne people know so well in winter. If the golden colour isn't enough to gladden the hearts of family and friends, then the wonderful aroma and flavour of the bread is sure to do so. Corn bread is best served and savoured as soon as it emerges from the oven, with a crisp, golden crust and cakey, crumbly texture. Try it with Chilli Beans (page 151) and a crisp leafy salad. For a sweet treat that's hard to beat, serve a sizzling skillet of corn bread with Raspberry Honey (page 68) — this makes a welcome change from the traditional Devonshire tea.

Method

Preheat the oven to 200°C/400°F.

Sift the polenta, flours, baking powder, bicarbonate of soda and salt in a large mixing bowl.

Place the yoghurt, honey and egg in a medium-sized mixing bowl and whisk together until well combined.

Heat a 23-cm (9-in) cast-iron frying pan (skillet) over a medium–high heat with the butter or oil.

Meanwhile, make a 'well' in the dry ingredients and pour in the yoghurt mixture.

Using a wooden spoon, work the dry ingredients lightly and quickly into the yoghurt mixture. The mixture should be of the consistency of a rather thick batter. Do not over mix or you will end up with pretty tough bread.

Pour the batter immediately into the hot frying pan until it bubbles up at the sides.

Place in the oven and bake for 25 minutes.

Serve sizzling hot, straight from the pan.

Ingredients

1 cup (175 g/6 oz) yellow polenta (cornmeal)

½ cup (75 g/2½ oz) wholemeal (wholewheat) flour

½ cup (75g/ 2½ oz) unbleached white flour

4 teaspoons baking powder

¼ teaspoon bicarbonate of soda (baking soda)

good pinch of salt

1½ cups (375 g/ 12 fl oz) plain yoghurt

1–2 tablespoons honey

1 egg, beaten lightly

2 teaspoons butter or oil

Serves 8

117

Speedy Couscous

Couscous, a popular ingredient in Middle Eastern cooking, is a type of fine semolina made from wheat grain. Traditionally, couscous required considerable preparation before it could be used in cooking. However, a pre-cooked variety is now available at supermarkets, delicatessens and health food stores; this type of couscous is wonderful to use because it can be cooked in minutes. Try using it as an alternative to rice, or as an accompaniment for tasty 'wet' dishes such as soups, stews and curries. Or mix it with a combination of diced or shredded vegetables, your favourite condiments, herbs and spices and you will have a delicious filling for pastry dishes and stuffed vegetables.

Pile freshly cooked couscous into bowls and top with hot vegetable or bean soups. It's terrific for whipping up quick salads too.

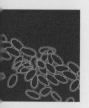

Method

Brush the base of a medium-sized saucepan with the oil, then add the couscous and cook over a medium-high heat for 2–3 minutes, stirring constantly. This roasts the couscous and imparts a sweet nutty flavour.

Add the water (or vegetable stock), cover and cook gently for 5 minutes.

Remove from the stove and allow to stand for 2–3 minutes before fluffing up the couscous with a fork.

Season to taste with the pepper.

Ingredients

1 teaspoon oil

2 cups (350 g/ 12 oz) couscous

2 cups (500 mL/ 16 fl oz) water *or* vegetable stock

pepper

Makes about 4 cups

Couscous with Vegies

A simple speedy dish that is similar to a pilaf. Serve it piled high with steamed vegetables with a bowl each of Quick Tomato Chutney (page 24) and yoghurt.

Ingredients

1 tablespoon olive oil

2 onions, diced or chopped finely, about 2 cups (300 g/10 oz)

1 capsicum (sweet pepper), seeded and diced, about 1½ cups (300 g/10 oz)

2 celery stalks, trimmed and diced

250 g (8 oz) green beans, trimmed and sliced

2 cups (350 g/ 12 oz) couscous

2 cups (500 mL/ 16 fl oz) vegetable stock

pepper

Serves 4

Method

Heat the oil in a medium-sized saucepan, then add the onion and stir over a medium heat for 1 minute.

Cover and cook for 5 minutes to cook the onion quickly.

Stir in the capsicum, celery and beans, then cover and cook for 3 minutes.

Add the couscous, then stir over the heat for 2–3 minutes.

Add the vegetable stock, then cover and cook gently for 5 minutes.

Remove from the stove and allow to stand for 2–3 minutes so that the couscous absorbs all the stock before seasoning to taste with the pepper.

Pancakes

Serve these hot, straight from the pan, or allow to cool and serve topped with Lemon Cream Cheese (page 184) and fresh fruit or fruit canned (tinned) in its own juice. For a special treat, spread with light cream cheese and Raspberry Honey (page 68).

Method

Ingredients

1½ cups (250 g/ 8 oz) wholemeal (wholewheat) self-raising flour

1 tablespoon sugar

1 egg

1¼ cups (310 mL/ 10 fl oz) milk

1 teaspoon vanilla essence (extract)

butter or oil for cooking

Makes about 12–15 pancakes, depending upon size of spoon

Using a food processor or blender, blend all the ingredients for 1 minute.

Allow to stand for 10–15 minutes, if possible, before cooking as this will soften the starch grains in the flour and ensure that the pancakes cook thoroughly.

Heat a frying pan (skillet) with a little of the butter (or oil) until quite hot.

Stir the mixture briskly and add 1 large serving spoonful at a time to the pan.

Cook until one side is a light golden-brown, about 1 minute, then flip over and cook until the other side is golden, about 30 seconds.

Stack the pancakes on a cake cooler topped with a clean dry tea towel until ready to eat.

These are like pikelets (also known as drop scones) and this is a great recipe to use both for savoury and sweet dishes. For a quick light meal or substantial snack, stack these pancakes on top of one another with layers of a tasty chutney and fresh tomatoes, then top with cheese and microwave on high for 1 minute. Alternatively, place the pancake stack in an ovenproof dish and bake in a preheated oven at 190°C/375°F for about 10 minutes, or until the cheese melts over the top. For a sweet treat, serve topped with Fresh Strawberry Sauce (page 71) with ice cream or pure cream nestling alongside.

Method

Using a food processor or blender, blend all the ingredients for 1 minute.

Allow to stand for 10–15 minutes, if possible, before cooking as this will soften the starch grains in the flour and ensure that the pancakes cook thoroughly.

Heat a frying pan (skillet) with a little oil (or butter) until quite hot.

Stir the pancake mixture briskly and add 1 large serving spoonful at a time to the pan.

Cook until one side is a light golden-brown, about 1 minute, then flip over and cook until the other side is golden, about 30 seconds.

Stack the pancakes on a cake cooler topped with a clean dry tea towel until ready to eat.

Ingredients

1 cup (155 g/5 oz) wholemeal (wholewheat) plain (all-purpose) flour

1 cup (125 g/4 oz) buckwheat flour

3 teaspoons baking powder

¼ teaspoon bicarbonate of soda (baking soda) dissolved in 2 tablespoons boiling water

1–2 eggs

1¼ cups (310 mL/ 11 fl oz) yoghurt or milk

butter or oil for cooking

Makes about 18 pancakes

Eggs are replaced with tofu in these pancakes which are served straight from the pan with a little honey. This is a great recipe when the pancake craving strikes but you are fresh out of eggs! Have a pack or two of UHT (Long Life) tofu on your pantry shelf for just this occasion.

Ingredients

1 cup (155 g/5 oz) wholemeal (wholewheat) self-raising flour

125 g (4 oz) tofu, drained

2 tablespoons sugar or 1 tablespoon honey

1 cup (250 mL/ 8 fl oz) soy milk

½ teaspoon vanilla essence (extract)

butter or oil for cooking

Makes about 8

Method

Place all the ingredients (except the butter or oil) in a food processor or blender and mix until a thick batter is produced.

Brush a frying pan (skillet) with a little melted butter (or oil) and preheat over a medium–high heat.

Add scant quarter cupfuls of the batter to the pan, allowing room between the pancakes so that they don't run into each other.

Cook each side until golden-brown. (Allow about 1 minute for one side, then 30 seconds for the other side.)

Repeat until all the mixture is used.

Oat and Honey Pancakes

A perfect dish for weekend breakfasts or winter desserts when more filling food is sought. Simply replace ½ cup of the flour with rolled oats in the Basic Pancake recipe and replace the sugar with honey.

Fantastic Filo (Phyllo)

Traditional use of filo pastry sees it doused in golden pools of melted butter, encasing savoury and sweet fillings alike. So, where does that leave the health-conscious person who loves these qualities but not the high fat content? I suggest you try the method outlined in the Vegetable Slice recipe (page 111). This way, the characteristic crispy texture and the golden colour of baked filo can be achieved with only a smidgen of fat.

A great nickname for ever-popular crêpes, this recipe is well worthwhile becoming familiar with. We use the name 'Skinny Pancakes' in our family to distinguish American-style pancakes from crêpes, and the name has stuck since my children were very young. Enjoy the versatility of Skinny Pancakes — they're a real taste treat when served drizzled with honey and lemon juice, rolled up and eaten straightaway. Or use to encase savoury or sweet fillings and serve as an entrée, main dish or dessert.

Method

Using a blender or food processor, blend all the ingredients except the butter together until well combined.

Allow to stand for 10–15 minutes, or up to an hour.

Heat a frying pan (skillet) with a little melted butter and cook the mixture over a medium heat in eighth-cupfuls for small pancakes and quarter-cupfuls for large pancakes.

When you add the mixture to the pan, rotate the pan and tilt it up and down to produce thin, even, round pancakes.

Cook for 30 seconds on one side, then carefully flip the pancake over and cook for 10 seconds or so on the other side.

Serve at once or allow to cool and store, covered, in the refrigerator until required.

Ingredients

1¼ cups (310 mL/ 10 fl oz) milk

1 egg

⅔ cup (85 g/3 oz) plain (all-purpose) flour

pinch of salt

a little butter

Makes 16 small or 8 large pancakes

Legumes & Nuts

Legendary

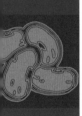

Legumes encompass a huge variety of beans, peas and lentils which are available from supermarkets, delicatessens and Asian grocery stores. In this book you'll find recipes using chick peas (garbanzo beans), red kidney, lima and cannellini beans and red and brown lentils. Even the humble baked bean gets a look in.

Don't be put off by the overly wholesome image that legumes have been tagged with in the past, for they are now appearing more frequently on the menus of many a bustling café and restaurant. Nowadays, as we enjoy food from many different cultures, we're more likely to be familiar with recipes which include legumes. Think of the last time you dipped some corn chips or pita bread into a bowl of houmus, or savoured spicy Mexican-style beans. Or even the last time you tucked into baked beans. These are all legumes, but there are many more dishes than these to explore. Enjoy trying Mediterranean-inspired dishes — Salad of White Beans (page 136) and Rich Red Bean Salad (page 132). Or have fun whipping up White Bean Purée (page 135) which is superb as a flavour-packed sandwich spread or dip.

Nuts and seeds are also foods which have been underrated and tarred with the high-fat brush. But look closer, and see how nuts and seeds can be incorporated into a range of delicious vegetable, pasta, noodle and legume dishes. Use them in a sensible proportion to these highly recommended foods and you will be able to benefit from the generous amounts of dietary fibre, calcium and protein they yield without overdoing your fat intake. Remember, the types of fat that nuts contain are largely polyunsaturated and mono-unsaturated, which are among the more recommended types of fat because they don't raise the body's blood cholesterol level as saturated fats do. So instead of eating copious amounts, enjoy nuts scattered as a garnish on your dishes.

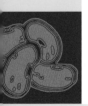

Legumes

Why are legumes held in such high regard by nutritionists? Because they are low in fat, high in dietary fibre and complex carbohydrate, contain good amounts of protein, iron and calcium and do not contain cholesterol. For the cook, they offer an exciting adventure, for they are very versatile foods which can be used in tasty dips and spreads, soups, salads, casseroles and hot pots. You would expect to pay handsomely for these attributes, but in fact legumes are inexpensive. Fortunately, we can now obtain a fair variety of canned beans and lentils, which cuts down on preparation of these dishes. However, you certainly have many more varieties available to you when you purchase the dried variety. And although the soaking and cooking process is not quick, it is easy and simple, and, to my mind, it is well worth while putting a little time aside now and then to soak and cook several batches of dried beans which can be stashed away in your freezer ready and waiting for a busy time, as outlined in the recipe for Basic Cooked Legumes (page 128).

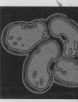

It is important to pre-soak most legumes, both to ensure that they can be cooked in a reasonable time and to render them digestible. I do not find this task either daunting or off-putting because it's just a matter of planning ahead. And that can be as simple as soaking whichever legumes you will need for the coming week as soon as you unpack your shopping. Do this in containers in the refrigerator, so that they don't spoil. The legumes can then be drained and either cooked straightaway or stored for later use. Even if you soak too many to use, don't worry. All you need to do is drain them and store them in containers in the freezer. This actually has a tenderising effect on the legumes. Cook the legumes when you are not too busy (I routinely do this while I am doing other things in the kitchen or around the house, for after the initial boiling, they require very little attention.) Once they are cooked, simply place the amount of cooked legumes you would normally use for a meal in an airtight storage container and store in the refrigerator for 5–7 days, or in the freezer for several weeks.

Method

Ingredients

2 cups (400 g/ 14 oz) dried beans, peas or lentils, rinsed and drained

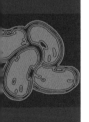

Makes about 4–5 cups (about 1½–2 kg/ 3½–4½ lb) cooked legumes

Place the legumes in a container, cover with 4 cups (1 litre/1¾ imp pints) cold water and cover with a lid.

Set aside to soak for 6–8 hours or overnight.

Drain the soaking water completely and place the legumes in a saucepan and cover with fresh cold water.

Bring the water to the boil and boil for 10 minutes, then reduce the heat and simmer, with the lid slightly ajar, until the legumes become quite tender. The legumes should be soft enough to be mashed with a fork. The length of cooking time for legumes varies according to their age — the older the legumes, the tougher they become and the longer they need to be cooked.

Another note — if you are going to add salt, do so at the end of the cooking. Adding salt in the beginning actually makes the legumes tough.

This is a life-saver, or, should I say, a 'meal saver', for those times when you want to use legumes in a special recipe but have forgotten to pre-soak them.

Method

Place the legumes in a stainless steel or enamel saucepan and add 4 cups (1 litre/1¾ imp pints) water.

Bring the mixture to the boil and boil for 3–5 minutes.

Remove from the heat, cover and set aside for about 30 minutes.

Drain the water and replace it with fresh water to cover and continue to cook as specified in your favourite recipes.

Ingredients

2 cups (400 g/ 14 oz) legumes, rinsed and drained

Makes about 4–5 cups (about 1½–2 kg/3½–4½ lb) cooked legumes

People constantly ask me for this recipe, and no wonder, for houmus is absolutely scrumptious and a real all-round favourite to serve when friends drop by. Dress it up by serving warmed pita bread wedges and, if you are looking for an accompaniment with a real crunch, Baked Mountain Bread (page 75). Serve a plate of seasonal vegetable titbits such as whole cherry or teardrop tomatoes, carrot rings or sticks, Blanched Broccoli (page 34) and some fresh leafy greens.

Method

Ingredients

2 cups (400 g/ 14 oz) cooked or canned (tinned) chick peas (garbanzo beans), drained

3 garlic cloves, crushed (pressed)

juice of 2 lemons, about 8 tablespoons

½ cup (125 mL/4 fl oz) vegetable stock

1–2 tablespoons soy sauce

2 tablespoons tahini (see right)

pepper

sweet paprika

1 tablespoon chopped parsley

Makes about 2½ cups (625 mL/ 20 fl oz)

Using a food processor with the metal chopping blade, process the chick peas until a fine meal is produced. Turn the processor off every now and then and scrape the sides of the bowl to make sure all the chick peas come in contact with the processor blade.

While the processor is operating, add the garlic, lemon juice, vegetable stock, soy sauce and tahini, then process until smooth.

Season to taste with the pepper, then place in a serving bowl and dust with the sweet paprika and sprinkle with the parsley.

Have You Tried Tahini?

Tahini is a creamy paste made from toasted sesame seeds which have been ground to a very fine meal and blended with a little sesame or peanut (groundnut) oil. Available from supermarkets and delicatessens, it is a popular ingredient in Mediterranean cooking where it is used extensively in dips, dressings and sauces.

Definitely a handy one to have in your repertoire, this dish can be used in so many ways — in nachos, tacos, as a filling for crepes or burritos, to pile on top of freshly cooked corn bread or grilled polenta (always have a dollop or two of sour cream or thick (Greek-style) yoghurt to go on top) and to complement a tasty salsa like Quick Red and Green Salsa (page 18) or Fresh Tomato Salsa (page 26).

Method

Heat the oil in a medium-large saucepan and stir-fry the onion, garlic, capsicum and chilli (or chilli powder) for 2 minutes.

Cover and cook over a medium heat for 5 minutes.

Add the tomato and tomato paste and cook, stirring, for 5 minutes.

Cover and simmer the mixture for 5 minutes, then add the kidney beans and simmer gently for about 10–15 minutes.

Season to taste with the pepper.

More Toppings for Chilli Beans

- strips of Roasted Capsicum (page 16)
- Chilli Tomato Sauce (page 25) for those who like it hot
- Avocado Hot Stuff (page 27)
- Coriander and Yoghurt Sauce (page 52)
- a dollop of thick (Greek-style) yoghurt and a large spoonful of Crunchy Red Cabbage Salad (page 46)

Ingredients

2 teaspoons olive oil

2 onions, diced finely, about 2 cups (300 g/10 oz)

2–3 garlic cloves, crushed (pressed)

1 red or green capsicum (sweet pepper), seeded and diced, about 1½ cups (300 g/10 oz)

1–2 teaspoons chopped seeded chillies (chilli peppers) or ½ teaspoon chilli powder

2 medium-large tomatoes, diced, about 2 cups (500 g/16 oz) or 425 g (15 oz) canned (tinned) tomatoes, chopped, juice included

2 tablespoons tomato paste (purée)

4 cups (800 g/ 1¾ lb) cooked or canned (tinned) red kidney beans, drained

pepper

Serves 6

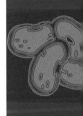

131

This delicious salad is a wonder to prepare if you have some canned or cooked red kidney beans on hand. The beautiful zesty flavour of lemons adds a real lift along with the 'oomph' of freshly crushed garlic and cracked black pepper. The colour of the red kidney beans is intensified by the addition of tomato paste and diced red capsicum.

Method

Ingredients

1 tablespoon olive oil

4 garlic cloves, crushed (pressed)

¼ teaspoon cracked black pepper

2 tablespoons tomato paste (purée)

juice of 1 lemon *or* lime, about 4 tablespoons, and 1 lemon, cut into wedges

3 cups (825 g/ 1¾ lb) cooked or canned (tinned) red kidney beans, drained

4 spring onions (scallions), finely sliced, green tops included

½ cup chopped coriander (cilantro) *or* parsley

¼ red capsicum (sweet pepper), seeded and diced finely, about ⅓ cup

Serves 4–6

Combine the oil, garlic, pepper, tomato paste and lemon (or lime) juice in a small bowl.

Add this mixture to the beans with the spring onion and most of the coriander (or parsley), and combine all the ingredients thoroughly.

Place the bean mixture in a serving bowl and serve topped with a small mound of diced capsicum and scattered with the remaining coriander (or parsley).

Serve with the lemon wedges.

Fresh Chillies — Hot Stuff!

When preparing fresh chillies (chilli peppers), do wear rubber gloves — the thin clingy type (not the roomy washing-up ones, otherwise it will be a bit like performing brain surgery with gardening gloves on!). The seeds and juices that are exuded when you cut chillies are extremely hot so avoid touching lips or eyes if you have even a trace of chilli on your hand, because the tender mucous membranes can be burned.

You can prepare fresh chillies ahead of time by slitting the pods open and gently scraping out the seeds using the tip of a small knife. Place the chilli flesh in a small jar and submerge in oil, then store in the refrigerator. The oil will become chilli-flavoured and can be used in cooking and dressings.

Fresh chillies can be roasted to subdue their burning properties; roasting also reduces their heat to the touch, preventing the juices from burning sensitive fingers when handling. Wash and dry the chillies and place them in a bowl. Drizzle a little oil over them and mix the chillies so that they are all coated in a thin layer of oil. Spread the chillies out on a baking tray (sheet) and bake at 180°C/350°F for 10 minutes. Allow to cool, then place the chillies in a jar and store them in the refrigerator for up to 1 week. To keep for longer, at room temperature, place the chillies in a jar and completely submerge in a good-quality oil.

For years we have 'poo-pooed' baked beans as a lowly food. But now that foods containing complex carbohydrates have been given the green flag, baked beans have climbed a few rungs on the meal rating ladder. They really are faster than the fast food that you have to queue up for, and contain virtually no fat, which is a far cry from what any fast food chain can claim. So, for a real fast — and wonderfully healthy — meal or snack, why not give baked beans a go, served on some good wholemeal or grain toast, or, to add a smidgen of finesse, try this dish.

Ingredients

1 x 810 g (1¾ lb) can (tin) baked beans

2 teaspoons olive oil

½ bunch spring onions (scallions), sliced, green tops included

1–2 red, yellow or green capsicums (sweet peppers), seeded and diced, about 2 cups (400 g/10 oz)

cracked black pepper

½ cup (60 g/2 oz) grated tasty (mature cheddar) cheese

1 quantity Fresh Tomato Salsa (page 26)

corn chips *or* toasted sliced breadstick

Serves 2–4

Method

Place the baked beans in a microwave-proof bowl, cover and cook on medium-high for 6 minutes.

If you don't have a microwave, place the beans in a medium-sized saucepan, cover and heat over a medium-high heat for about 10 minutes, stirring occasionally to prevent the beans from catching on the base of the pan.

Meanwhile, heat the oil in a frying pan (skillet) and stir in the spring onion and capsicum, cooking gently for 1 minute. Then place the lid on the pan and cook for 3–4 minutes.

Sprinkle with cracked black pepper.

Stir half this mixture into the beans.

To assemble the dish, place the beans in serving bowls, then sprinkle over the grated cheese.

Top with the remaining capsicum mixture, then the Fresh Tomato Salsa. Arrange corn chips (or toasted sliced breadstick) around the bowls and serve.

Serve this delicious purée with fresh wholemeal, grain or rye bread and fresh sun-ripened tomatoes and cracked black pepper. It is wonderful for dipping too, so serve with some Baked Mountain Bread (page 75) or wedges of pita bread with fresh and blanched vegetables.

Method

Place the beans in a food processor with the metal chopping blade and blend until smooth, adding the garlic and oil while the processor is operating.

If the mixture is too dry (it should be rather like houmus dip, but thicker), add a little vegetable stock (or the liquid in which the beans have been cooked).

Season to taste with the salt and pepper.

Ingredients

2 cups (400 g/ 14 oz) canned (tinned) or pre-cooked canellini beans (page 128) or lima beans, drained

2–3 garlic cloves, crushed (pressed)

2 tablespoons extra virgin olive oil

3 tablespoons vegetable stock or bean cooking liquid, if needed

salt and pepper

Makes about 2 cups

This is a lovely quick salad that is both tasty and surprisingly filling. I like using canellini beans because of their soft creamy texture but lima or Great Northern beans are good alternatives. This dish is perfect for serving at the end of summer when capsicums (sweet peppers) are still in their seasonal glory and rich red sun-ripened tomatoes are easy to come by.

Method

Ingredients

2 cups (250 g/8 oz) sliced button mushrooms

1 large red capsicum (sweet pepper), cut into four and seeded

4 firm but ripe tomatoes, diced, about 4 cups (1 kg/2¼ lb)

4 tablespoons extra virgin olive oil

4–6 garlic cloves (or more if you are game, like me!), chopped

1 tablespoon fresh or 2 teaspoons dried oregano

4 cups (800 g/ 1¾ lb) cooked canellini or lima beans

½ cup chopped parsley

salt and pepper

Serves 6

136

Place the mushrooms, capsicum and tomato in a large mixing bowl, and decant the beans into another bowl.

Place the oil, garlic and oregano in a small saucepan and heat gently for 1 minute, to soften the flavour of the garlic.

Drizzle this mixture over the beans and fold through, taking care not to break them up.

Then fold the mushroom mixture through the beans with most of the parsley, and season to taste with the salt and pepper.

Transfer the salad to a serving bowl and scatter with the remaining parsley.

Fleshy Tomatoes for Salads and Sandwiches

Choose tomatoes that have plenty of flesh rather than too many juicy seeds for salads such as Salad of White Beans (this page). I like using Roma (plum) tomatoes, but my favourite full-flavoured tomatoes for this dish (and for slicing thickly for sandwiches) are beefsteak tomatoes which sound like a real contradiction of terms for a vegetarian cook! Do look out for these wonderful buxom, flavour-packed tomatoes. They are not as widely available as the more common varieties, but well worth the search; you could even acquire your own seedlings to plant in the garden or in large pots.

Burgers, it seems, are here to stay. And favourites like lentil burgers seem to be no exception in spite of the 'hippie food' tag they collected in the 70s. These days, however, you will be more likely to find them used as a filling for fresh or toasted foccacia bread along with a spicy salsa and tender greens rather than on a bun with a clump of alfalfa sprouts and grated carrot. Try these burgers with one or more of the tasty salsas or salads listed below.

If you have a food processor, you'll be able to save plenty of time by using the metal chopping blade to chop the parsley, onions and carrot. These need to be chopped finely so that the burgers hold together and the vegetables cook through.

Method

If you have a food processor, process the parsley (or coriander), onions and carrot.

Then add all the ingredients, except for the flour and oats, to a large mixing bowl and combine well.

Add the flour and enough oats to bring the mixture to a burger consistency.

Form the mixture into burgers and cook until golden brown (about 3 or 4 minutes each side) in a little oil in a hot frying pan.

Drain well and serve at once or refrigerate or freeze until required.

Ingredients

½ bunch Italian parsley *or* coriander (cilantro), chopped finely

1–2 onions, diced finely, about 2 cups (300 g/10 oz)

1 large carrot, scrubbed and grated

1 egg beaten *or* 60 g (2 oz) tofu, mashed

pepper

3 tablespoons crunchy peanut butter

3 tablespoons soy sauce

3 cups (600 g/1¼ lb) cooked brown lentils *or* red kidney beans, drained well

2 tablespoons wholemeal (wholewheat) flour

about 1 cup (150 g/ 5 oz) quick cooking oats

about 2 tablespoons oil for cooking

Makes about 16

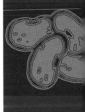

Salads, Sauces and Salsas for Lentil Burgers

- Scarlet Sauce (page 17)
- Quick Tomato Chutney (page 24)
- Quick Red and Green Salsa (page 18)
- Chilli Tomato Sauce (page 25)
- Avocado Hot Stuff (page 27)
- Ruby Red Salad (page 44)
- Red Cabbage Pickle (page 45)
- Crunchy Red Cabbage Salad (page 46)

Make more of this delicious dish than you need because some can be frozen for a quick meal when you have no time for cooking. Serve with Couscous (page 119), rice or fresh crusty bread.

Ingredients

1 tablespoon olive oil

1–2 onions, diced, about 2 cups (300 g/10 oz)

3 large carrots, scrubbed and diced

3–4 garlic cloves, crushed (pressed)

1–2 teaspoons finely sliced or chopped, seeded chillies (chilli peppers)

¼ cauliflower, cut into large florets, stalk cut into chunks

1 cup (250 g/8 oz) green beans, topped and tailed and cut in half

2 cups (400 g/ 14 oz) split red lentils, soaked and drained

2–3 cups (500–750 mL/ 16–24 fl oz) vegetable stock

cracked black pepper

Serves 6

Method

Heat the oil in a large saucepan and stir-fry the onion and carrot for 2 minutes.

Cover and cook over low-medium heat for 5 minutes.

Add the garlic, chilli, cauliflower and green beans, stir through, then cover and cook for 2 minutes.

Add the lentils and stock and bring the braise to the boil. Reduce the heat, cover and cook for 20 minutes, stirring from time to time.

Season to taste with the pepper and serve piping hot.

A Note on Soaking Red Lentils

Split red lentils require less soaking and cooking than any other legume, but soaking them for about 2 hours helps to reduce the whole cooking time for this recipe.

The wonderful golden colour and sweet flavour of these burgers is imparted by the onion, carrot and pumpkin (or sweet potato). These luscious burgers are especially good served with full-flavoured, bitter or peppery greens such young spinach leaves, the inner leaves of curly endive, radicchio or rocket (arugula). Add a blast of flavour by serving them with any of the sauces, salsas or salads listed on page 137.

Method

Heat 1 tablespoon of the oil in a large saucepan and stir-fry the onion over a medium heat for 1 minute.

Stir in the celery, carrots and pumpkin (or sweet potato) and cover and cook for 10 minutes.

Add the lentils and vegetable stock and bring the mixture to the boil, stirring to prevent the mixture catching on the bottom of the pan. Reduce the heat to medium, then cover and cook for 15 minutes, or until the vegetables can be mashed with a fork.

Remove from the heat, then stir in the spring onion, parsley, soy sauce and pepper. Combine all the ingredients well, then transfer the mixture to a large heatproof bowl to allow it to cool more quickly.

When the mixture is warm, stir in enough wheat germ to bring the mixture to a soft, dough-like consistency, then, using your hands, form the mixture into burgers.

Using a pastry brush, brush the base of a large frying pan (skillet) with a little oil and heat over a medium-high heat.

Cook 5 burgers at a time for 2 minutes each side, or until they become golden-brown, adding 1 tablespoon of oil to the pan before cooking each new batch.

Ingredients

3 tablespoons oil

1 onion, diced, about 1 cup (150 g/5 oz)

1 stalk celery, trimmed and diced finely

2 carrots, scrubbed and chopped

500 g (1 lb) pumpkin or sweet potato, peeled and cut into chunks

2 cups (400 g/ 14 oz) pre-soaked red lentils, drained

1 cup (250 mL/ 8 fl oz) vegetable stock

6 spring onions (scallions), sliced, green tops included

1 cup chopped parsley

2 tablespoons soy sauce

¼ teaspoon cracked black pepper

1 cup (90 g/3 oz) wheat germ or 1 cup (150 g/5 oz) quick cooking oats

Makes about 15

139

Nuts

There has long been a love affair between the northern African people and peanuts, or groundnuts as they are also called. Handfuls of these pounded nuts are added to soups and stews for their thickening properties as well as flavour. Peanuts are actually categorised as a legume rather than as a nut, but I have placed them amongst other nuts because that is the way we generally think of them. Compared to other legumes, peanuts are relatively high in fat, but I can always find a place for these nutritious foods in my repertoire of dishes. Simply balance rich foods like nut-filled sauces with plenty of vegetables, noodles, bread or rice, and you have a well-balanced meal! A perfect example of this is serving a Vegetable Platter (page 47) with Quick Satay Sauce (page 142) and Baked Mountain Bread (page 75) or Braised Tofu (page 164) with a bowl of steaming noodles and Crunchy Peanut Salsa (see opposite).

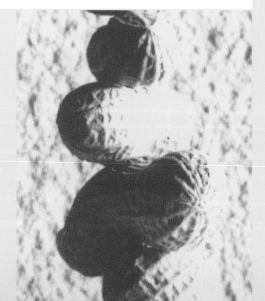

A beautiful fragrant dish with a satisfying crunch. Enjoy serving it with chapatis or Baked Mountain Bread (page 75) or spooned over soups and casseroles for a tasty and colourful garnish.

Method

Heat the oil in a medium-sized saucepan, then add the onion, stirring over the heat for 1 minute.

Stir in the garlic and chilli, then add the peanuts, tomato and spring onion and cover and cook for 5 minutes.

Remove from the heat and stir in the lime juice and pepper to taste.

Serve at room temperature sprinkled with coriander (or parsley).

Ingredients

2 teaspoons sesame oil

1 onion, diced, about 1 cup (150 g/5 oz)

2–3 garlic cloves, crushed (pressed)

1 teaspoon finely sliced or diced, seeded red or green chillies (chilli peppers)

1 cup (150 g/5 oz) dry roasted peanuts (groundnuts)

1 tomato, diced, about 1 cup (250 g/8 oz)

6–8 spring onions (scallions), sliced, green tops included

juice of 1 lime, about 4 tablespoons

pepper

3 tablespoons chopped coriander (cilantro) or parsley

Makes about 3 cups (750 mL/24 fl oz)

When I say quick, I'm not kidding. This recipe is a real winner with vegetables and rice or noodles, or if you simply want a tasty sauce to serve alongside crispy vegetable crudites for an appetiser or snack.

Ingredients

1 teaspoon sesame oil

2 garlic cloves, crushed (pressed)

1 teaspoon finely chopped, seeded red or green chillies (chilli peppers)

2 cups (500 mL/ 16 fl oz) vegetable stock

2 tablespoons tomato paste (purée)

½ cup (125 g/4 oz) crunchy peanut butter

1 tablespoon soy sauce

pepper

Makes about 2 cups (500 mL/16 fl oz)

Method

Heat the oil in a small saucepan and lightly cook the garlic and chilli, taking care not to burn them.

Remove from the heat and stir in the vegetable stock, tomato paste and peanut butter.

Return to the heat and bring the mixture to the boil, then reduce the heat and simmer, stirring occasionally, for 10 minutes.

Season with the soy sauce and pepper.

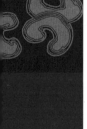

Here you are, Jacqui and Scott — the recipe you have been waiting for! Nutty pizzas? Yes, nuts go especially well with vegie pizzas, say my pals and recipe taste testers. Serve each pizza topped with a generous dollop of Chunky Cucumber Dip (page 175) and Fresh Tomato Salsa (page 26) with a fresh crisp salad.

Method

Preheat the oven to 200°C/400°F.

Cut the muffins in half, then spread the Satay Sauce on each half.

Scatter the capsicum, beanshoots, sweet corn, tomato, peanuts and spring onion over.

Bake in a hot oven for 10–12 minutes.

Ingredients

6 English-style muffins

1 quantity Quick Satay Sauce (page 142)

½ red capsicum (sweet pepper), seeded and sliced, about ¾ cup (150 g/5 oz)

1 cup (125 g/4 oz) beanshoots

1 cup (175 g/6 oz) sweet corn kernels

3 firm but ripe tomatoes, diced, about 3 cups (750 g/1½ lb)

⅔ cup (90 g/3 oz) dry roasted peanuts (groundnuts)

2 spring onions, (scallions), finely sliced, green tops included

Makes 12

A delightful dip with a truly scrumptious flavour. Serve with corn chips or crackers and a selection of fresh seasonal vegetables. It's perfect for piping mini swirls on top of crackers or pumpernickel rounds for finger foods. Or use it as a tasty filling for sandwiches such as Mountain Bread Roll-ups (page 76).

Method

Ingredients

1 cup (150 g/5 oz) cashews, roasted (page 108)

125 g (4 oz) cream cheese or soft tofu, drained

2 garlic cloves, crushed (pressed)

juice of 1 lemon, about 4 tablespoons

3 tablespoons yoghurt or vegetable stock

cracked black pepper or sweet paprika

Makes about 1 cup

Using a food processor, blend all the ingredients except the pepper (or paprika) together until smooth.

Transfer to a serving bowl and serve, dusted with cracked black pepper (or sweet paprika).

These biscuits are a little higher in fat and sugar than the recipes I usually create, but they are meant for special occasions. They were inspired by the news of the birth of a daughter — C.C. — to my friends Broni and Neil. I just had to cook something to celebrate, so what better than sweet treats in the shape of hearts!

Method

Using a food processor with the metal chopping blade, grind the almonds to a meal.

Add the butter, bit by bit, and then the sugar and the lemon rind and juice.

Sift the flours and baking powder, then add to the processor.

Remove and place the mixture in a plastic bag and chill in the refrigerator for 1 hour.

Roll the mixture out between two pieces of baking paper (to prevent it sticking to the bench and the rolling pin) to a $^1/_2$-cm ($^1/_{10}$-in) thickness. Using a biscuit-cutter (heart-shaped or stars), cut the mixture into shapes and place on baking trays that have been topped with baking paper.

Bake at 180°C/350°F for 12–15 minutes. The biscuits should be a light golden–brown colour when cooked.

Allow to cool for 5 minutes, then transfer to a cake cooler.

When completely cold, you can decorate with icing if desired. I continued in celebratory spirit by piping C.C. on to each biscuit and adding tiny silver, gold and pink balls for decoration.

Ingredients

1 cup (155 g/5 oz) almonds

½ cup (125 g/4 oz) butter

¾ cup (115 g/4 oz) icing sugar

finely grated rind of 1 lemon

juice of ½ lemon, about 2 tablespoons

½ cup (90 g/3 oz) rice flour

½ cup (60 g/2 oz) unbleached white (all-purpose) flour

2 teaspoons baking power

Makes about 30 biscuits

Terrific

Tofu & Soy Foods

The soy bean is often referred to as the 'miracle bean' because it contains all the amino acids essential for the growth, maintenance and repair of our bodies.
I have a real passion for tofu, my favourite of all soy foods so I've given it a whole chapter to itself.

This statement usually catches people by surprise because tofu, in its natural state, would have to be one of the most bland foods around. This, however, is just the reason I love working with tofu — because it lends itself to teaming up with a host of hot, spicy, sweet and savoury ingredients and can be used to make a range of dishes from soups and starters to desserts and cakes.

There are so many foods derived from the soy bean, from increasingly popular soy drink — perfect for finishing off blended soups because it lends them a sweet nutty flavour and a surprisingly creamy texture — and tofu (otherwise known as bean curd), tempeh (cakes of fermented soy beans) to soy 'cheese' to roasted soy bean 'nuts' that seem to have hit the healthy snack market by storm. Soy foods have been well received by modern consumers on the lookout for healthier products, especially those products which are low in fat and contain virtually no cholesterol.

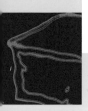

Super Soy Beans

Dried soy beans can be cooked as in the recipe for Basic Cooked Legumes (page 128) and incorporated in a variety of dishes such as soups, stews and hot pots, sweet and sour dishes and salads. Soy burgers are popular and can be whipped up from cooked ground soy beans with vegetables and rice. You can even substitute ground cooked soy beans for the lentils in All-time-favourite Lentil Burgers (page 137) or Red Lentil and Vegetable Burgers (page 139).

To Grind Soy Beans

Cook soy beans as for Basic Cooked Legumes (page 128) and drain them thoroughly. Or use canned (tinned), well-drained soy beans. Using your food processor with the metal chopping blade, grind the beans until they reach the desired consistency. Use a scraper to prevent the beans becoming caked on the sides of the processor bowl so that they all come in contact with the metal blade. Or, use Cooked Soy Grits (see page 150) as a base for tasty burgers and salads.

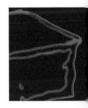

Soy grits are a really convenient way for the busy person to incorporate soy beans in their meal time repertoire. Readily available in the health food section of supermarkets and at health food stores, soy grits are roasted soy beans which have been ground to a coarse meal. It is an inexpensive food which can be used in place of burghul wheat, rice or couscous for all manner of dishes including stuffings for baked vegetables.

Method

Ingredients

2 cups (375 g/ 13 oz) soy grits

3 cups (750 mL/ 24 fl oz) vegetable stock or water

pinch of salt (optional)

Makes about 5 cups (925 g/2 lb)

Place the grits, stock (or water) and salt (if using) in a medium-sized saucepan and bring the mixture to the boil. Reduce the heat immediately to prevent the grits from boiling over.

Cook gently for 12–15 minutes or until the grits are tender and can be mashed with a fork.

Make sure you drain them thoroughly if you are going to keep them for any length of time in the refrigerator because dry cooked grits have a much longer shelf life.

A quick and tasty accompaniment for hot spicy dishes or for serving cold as a salad. And great served as a sandwich filling for pita bread or Mountain Bread Roll-ups (page 76).

Method

Heat the oil in a large saucepan and stir-fry the onion over a medium heat for 1 minute, then cover and cook for 5 minutes.

Stir in the celery stalks, garlic, capsicum, mushrooms, tomato, grits and stock.

Bring the mixture to the boil, stirring every now and then to make sure it doesn't catch on the base of the pan.

Once boiling, reduce the heat immediately and cook the pilaf gently for 15 minutes.

Season to taste with the pepper and, if using, the soy sauce.

Serve sprinkled with the chopped celery leaves.

Ingredients

2–3 teaspoons olive oil

2 onions, diced finely, about 2 cups (300 g/10 oz)

2 celery stalks, trimmed and diced

2–3 garlic cloves, crushed (pressed)

1 capsicum (sweet pepper), seeded and diced, about 1½ cups (300 g/10 oz)

1 cup (125 g/4 oz) sliced button mushrooms

1 medium-large ripe tomato, diced, about 1 cup (275 g/ 10 oz) or 1 cup canned (tinned) crushed tomatoes

2 cups (375 g/ 13 oz) soy grits

3 cups (750 mL/ 24 fl oz) vegetable stock

pepper

1 tablespoon soy sauce (optional)

½ cup finely chopped celery leaves

Serves 4

Tofu

Otherwise known as bean curd, tofu has been used for centuries by the Chinese and Japanese. If you have never been a tofu lover, I hope the recipes in this book will change your mind, even if you try recipes in which tofu is not apparent, such as Quick Corn Bread (page 117), Soy Pancakes (page 122) and Fruity Blissballs (page 60). In fact, tofu makes a great substitute for eggs in cake, pancake and waffle recipes.

There are several types of tofu available. Firm or dried tofu has a solid texture and is suitable for a wide range of uses, but is especially suited to grilling (broiling), roasting and stir-frying. Do not confuse this dried tofu with the freeze-dried tofu described below. Dried tofu is easily cut into cubes or slices because it retains its shape well. Regular tofu has a softer texture, yet is still suitable for roasting and grilling. However, it needs to be drained well and the excess moisture pressed out before it can stand up well to the rigours of stir-frying.

Silken tofu, as the name implies, has a rather fragile, smooth texture and therefore lends itself well to dishes such as dips, dressings, cheesecakes, ice cream and other whipped desserts and toppings. Freeze-dried tofu has an almost blotting-paper-like texture. It is very porous and when soaked in water or a marinade, reconstitutes quite quickly. Tofu is available from Asian grocery stores, health food stores and supermarkets.

An all-time favourite of mine because it is a quick and easy recipe that is delicious and nutritious as well. Try serving it with falafels, corn chips, warm pita bread or a colourful selection of crisp vegetable crudites. All of the types of tofu mentioned on the previous page, with the exception of freeze-dried tofu, can be used for this recipe.

Method

Place the tofu, garlic, lemon juice, tahini, soy sauce and yoghurt into a food processor and blend until smooth.

Season to taste with the Tabasco Sauce and pepper.

Ingredients

250 g (8 oz) tofu, drained

2–3 garlic cloves, crushed (pressed)

juice of 1 lemon, about 4 tablespoons

2 tablespoons tahini

1 tablespoon soy sauce

2–3 tablespoons yoghurt

few drops Tabasco Sauce

pepper

Makes about 1½ cups (280 g/ 10 oz)

The versatility of tofu shines through in creamy dishes like this one which can be whipped up instantly using a food processor.

Ingredients

250 g (8 oz) soft tofu, drained

3–4 tablespoons yoghurt *or* **soy drink**

1–2 garlic cloves, crushed (pressed)

juice of ½ lemon, about 2 tablespoons

1 tablespoon tahini

¼ teaspoon ground cumin

salt and pepper

2 tablespoons finely sliced chives *or* **chopped coriander (cilantro)**

Makes about 1½ cups (375 mL/ 12 fl oz)

Method

Using a food processor, blend all the ingredients except for the chives (or coriander) together until smooth and creamy. Use a scraper to incorporate any ingredients that adhere to the sides of the food processor to make sure they all get a good blending.

Transfer the dressing to a serving dish and scatter the chives (or coriander) over.

I just had to include this dip here because miso is prepared from soy beans too (see page 161). Serve with a platter of crisp cooked seasonal vegetables for a warming treat. This dip makes a great sandwich spread and is delicious spread on top of firm drained tofu and eaten at once, or dressed up, as for Tofu Canapes (page 162).

I like to make at least twice the quantity of Sweet & Sour Miso Dip because it also doubles as a marvellous marinade for tofu. Use left-over dip to spread onto slices of firm, drained tofu, then put into a storage container and refrigerate for a day or so. Then, when required, bake as for Tofu Chilli Bake (page 158), popping some vegetables in the oven to bake at the same time.

Method

Using a wooden spoon, combine all the ingredients in a small bowl.

If you do not intend to use it at once, store this dip in an airtight container in the refrigerator for up to 1 week.

Ingredients

4 tablespoons white miso

2 teaspoons honey

1 tablespoon rice or white wine vinegar

2 tablespoons soy sauce

2 teaspoons grated ginger

2 garlic cloves, crushed (pressed)

½ cup (125 mL/ 4 fl oz) vegetable stock

Makes about 1 cup (250 mL/8 fl oz)

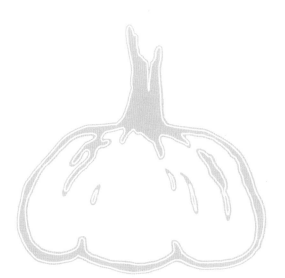

This recipe for tasty tofu is deliberately designed to make plenty of servings just because it has so many uses. It is great served with roasted vegetables which can be cooked in the oven at the same time as the tofu. Served hot or cold, it makes a delicious filling for wholemeal or multi-grain rolls. Once cooked and cooled, the tofu becomes quite firm and is perfect added to stir-fried vegetables, noodles, rice or antipasto platters. As for Tofu Chilli Bake (see page 158), it can be prepared ahead of time for convenience.

Ingredients

750 g (1¾ lb) tofu, drained

½ teaspoon peanut (groundnut) or sesame oil

1 quantity Quick Satay Sauce (page 142)

3–4 tablespoons chopped parsley or coriander (cilantro) for garnishing

Serves 6–8

Method

Preheat the oven to 200°C/400°F.

Cut the tofu into slices approximately 1 cm (½ in) thick and place them on a baking tray (sheet) which has been brushed with oil.

Spread the Satay Sauce over the tofu slices and bake them in a moderately hot oven for 20–25 minutes.

Garnish with the parsley (or coriander).

Soy 'Cheese'

Soy 'cheese' is manufactured from soy beans and is generally free of lactose (the sugar component of milk which some people cannot tolerate). It is not purely dairy free because some brands contain casein, a protein constituent of cow's milk. However, it is well worth noting that, as for soy drink, soy cheese contains largely polyunsaturated fats and no cholesterol. Try using it for cheese sauces, or for topping scrumptious baked casseroles like Tofu Chilli Bake (page 158), lasagne or even pizza. Plain and flavoured varieties are available, so have fun trying both.

Soy 'Nuts'

Soy 'nuts' are roasted flavoured soy beans. Because they are prepared purely from soy beans, they are a good substitute for peanuts (groundnuts) for those wishing to reduce their fat intake, or people with allergies to peanuts. Be sure to check the details of the composition of the soy nuts you intend to buy if you are allergic to peanuts — some brands add peanut flavour from peanuts themselves. Soy nuts have about half the fat of nuts like peanuts, almonds, cashews and walnuts, and are high in complex carbohydrate and dietary fibre. They are great for adding to salads, scattering over cooked pasta and vegetable dishes; in fact, you can use them in any recipe in place of nuts. You can even use them to make Crunchy Peanut Salsa (page 141), but then you would have to change the name to Crunchy Soy 'Nut' Salsa!

Soy nuts are also available in a scrumptious peanut-butter-like spread. You can use it wherever you would use peanut butter, such as in sandwiches, on toast and in peanut sauces and dips. It even stands alone as a dip, for serving with crisp carrot sticks or Blanched Broccoli florets (page 34). Try it in Quick Satay Sauce in place of the peanut butter for a reduced-fat version of this delicious recipe.

Tofu *Chilli* Bake

Many people find the bland flavour of tofu off-putting, but not me! I have fun dressing it up with flavours to suit the occasion, weather, or simply the accompaniments I wish to serve with it. In this recipe I have chosen the heat of chillies and the robust flavour of garlic and tomatoes. Serve it as it is with roasted potatoes and pumpkin in the winter months, or new season's asparagus and honeyed baby carrots in spring and summer. For a light meal, try it with alfalfa and radish sprouts as a wonderful and substantial filling for crusty rolls or warmed pita pocket bread.

You can prepare this dish ahead of time up to the stage of sprinkling the cheese on top. Cover and store in the refrigerator for up to three days, which helps the flavour infuse through the tofu. Then, when required, top with the cheese and bake as described below.

Method

Ingredients

500 g (1 lb) firm tofu, drained

a little olive oil

1 cup Quick & Tasty Pasta Sauce (page 91) *or* a good brand-name of bottled pasta sauce

1–2 teaspoons good commercial brand of garlic and chilli sauce

1 cup (125 g/4 oz) grated tasty (mature cheddar) cheese, *or* soy 'cheese' (see page 157)

cracked black pepper

2–3 tablespoons chopped parsley *or* coriander (cilantro)

Serves 4–6

Preheat the oven to 200°C/400°F.

Cut the tofu into 1-cm (½-in) slices and place them in a single layer in a baking dish that has been brushed with a little oil.

Combine the Pasta Sauce with the garlic and chilli sauce, then spread the mixture over the tofu.

Sprinkle with the cheese and cracked black pepper and bake in a hot oven for 20–25 minutes or until the tofu has become golden-brown.

Sprinkle with the parsley (or coriander) and serve at once or allow to cool, then refrigerate until required.

158

Scatter these over soups or salads and add to sandwiches, particularly Mountain Bread Roll-ups (page 76). The beauty of these croutons is that they are oven-roasted rather than deep-fried and are therefore much lower in fat. They also add more substance to quick dishes, for tofu is surprisingly satisfying. They take about 5 minutes to prepare and 15 minutes to roast, so you could whip up a quick soup while they were baking, or assemble a salad of greens, Blanched Broccoli (page 34) and even roast some capsicums. If roasted cashews sound good to serve scattered over your salad, pop some in the oven while the tofu croutons are roasting (see page 108 for how to roast nuts).

Method

Preheat the oven to 220°C/425°F.

Using a pastry brush, brush a baking tray (sheet) with a little of the oil.

Using a clean dry tea towel, pat the tofu dry, then cut it into 1-cm (½-in) cubes and place them in a large bowl.

Combine the soy sauce, spring onion tops (or chives), garlic (if using) and the remaining oil.

Sprinkle the mixture over the tofu, then, using your hands, mix all the ingredients well to ensure that the tofu is coated with the soy mixture.

Spread the tofu croutons out on the prepared baking tray and bake them in a hot oven for 15 minutes.

Ingredients

2 teaspoons sesame oil

500 g (1 lb) firm tofu, drained well

2 tablespoons soy sauce

1 tablespoon finely sliced spring onion tops _or_ chives

1 garlic clove, crushed (pressed) (optional)

Serves 6

Sushi rolls are a real winner for quick snacks and light meals. Serve with Sweet Chilli Sauce (page 53) or Garlic and Ginger Sauce (page 51).

Method

Ingredients

4 toasted nori sheets (page 104)

4 teaspoons white miso

4 teaspoons tahini

375 g (13 oz) firm tofu, drained, cut into thin sticks

1 carrot, scrubbed and cut into thin sticks

60 g (2 oz) pickled daikon radish, cut into thin sticks

4 tablespoons shredded pickled ginger or Red Cabbage Pickle (page 45)

4 cups mixed salad greens, chopped roughly

Makes about 24 slices

Lay the nori sheets on a clean bench top or wooden board.

Spread 1 teaspoon of the miso and 1 teaspoon of the tahini over each nori sheet.

Arrange the sticks of tofu, carrot and daikon radish along the edge of the nori closest to you.

Arrange a narrow row of pickled ginger (or Red Cabbage Pickle) alongside, then top all with the chopped greens.

Using a pastry brush, brush the edge of the nori furthest from you with a little water.

Applying firm pressure, roll the nori up in a cylindrical fashion to form a firm roll. Continue with all the nori sheets and vegetables.

Then, using a sharp knife, cut the rolls into 6 neat slices and arrange on a large serving platter or individual plates.

Miso

Miso is made from fermented soy beans, usually with the addition of a grain such as rice or barley. Miso generally has a full-bodied, salty flavour. The flavour of different types of miso varies in intensity according to the ingredients used and the length of fermentation time. I really like using white miso (also known as shiro miso, or young rice miso) for general use. Containing less than half the salt content of other miso, white miso has a rather sweet nutty flavour, and, used as it is, makes a wonderful spread for sandwiches or nori rolls. To make a delicious light vegetable stock from white miso, simply blend 2 teaspoons miso gradually into 1 cup boiling water.

Other popular varieties of miso are hatcho and mugi miso. They are fermented for longer than white miso and so develop a stronger, more full-bodied flavour. A more hearty vegetable stock can be made from them — just blend a level teaspoon of hatcho or mugi miso into 1 cup boiling water.

Healthy Tips for Deep-frying

Begin by using good-quality oil rather than animal fat as polyunsaturated and mono-unsaturated oils help reduce the body's blood cholesterol level and therefore help reduce heart disease. Peanut (groundnut) oil is frequently used for deep frying because it has a high smoking point.

The temperature at which food is fried is important. Frying at the correct temperature can make the difference between crisp light food and dull heavy food. Firstly, make sure the oil is hot enough before you add the food, otherwise more oil will be absorbed into the food before the surface is sealed. As soon as the food is cooked, remove it immediately and drain thoroughly. For small pieces of food, first drain the excess oil, then pop a few, a serve at a time, into a brown paper bag and give it a good shake. You will notice the paper becoming translucent as it absorbs the oil.

Broni, this recipe is for you, oh lover of coriander (cilantro) and wasabi and other things grand! These delightful little taste treats are wonderful for serving chilled in hot weather when their flavour-packed ingredients act as an appetiser. Serve them as a finger food at social gatherings, or make a meal out of them with some sushi rolls and tasty dipping sauces. Try extending your own creativity with imaginative toppings (see below).

Method

Ingredients

500 g (1 lb) firm tofu, drained

1 tablespoon white miso or Sweet & Sour Miso Dip (page 155)

1 teaspoon wasabi paste

½ sheet toasted nori (page 104)

Wrap the tofu in a clean dry tea towel and press firmly to remove any excess moisture.

Unwrap the tofu and, using a sharp knife, cut across horizontally in three layers.

Spread the first layer with white miso (or Sweet and Sour Miso Dip). Spread the second layer with wasabi paste. Top the third layer with the toasted nori.

Cut each layer into neat 2-cm (¾-in) squares, rectangles or triangles.

Arrange on a serving platter or individual plates and top with your choice of the toppings below. Or try stacking two or three layers on top of one another.

Serves 4–6

Toppings for Tofu Canapes

shredded pickled ginger

Red Cabbage Pickle (page 45)

Quick Pickled Carrots (page 32)

chopped coriander (cilantro)

diced pickled daikon radish

fine slivers of red capsicum (sweet pepper)

Quick and easy to prepare, Crispy Tofu can be used as the basis of many a dish. Try it added to stir-fried vegetables, rice or noodle dishes, soups, or even scattered over soups as croutons. It is especially delicious served with Quick Satay Sauce (page 142). Its possibilities go on and on. Just change the size and shape of the tofu to suit the recipe.

Method

Place the tofu in a bowl.

Combine the soy sauce, mirin (or wine or fruit juice) and garlic and drizzle over the tofu.

Carefully toss the tofu to allow it to become coated with the marinade. Cover and allow to stand for at least 1 hour, or preferably all day in the refrigerator.

Combine the flour and polenta and coat the tofu cubes with the mixture.

Heat the oil in a deep frying pan (skillet) or wok. You can test if it is hot enough for cooking the tofu by dropping in a cube of bread — when it rises to the surface and quickly becomes golden-brown, the oil is ready.

Fry the tofu until golden-brown, then immediately remove it from the oil, using a slotted spoon.

Drain thoroughly on paper towels and/or brown paper bags (see page 161 for Healthy Tips for Deep-frying) and serve hot.

Ingredients

500 g (1 lb) firm tofu, cut into cubes, slices or strips

2 tablespoons soy sauce

1 tablespoon mirin *or sweet white wine or fruit juice*

2 garlic cloves, crushed (pressed)

3 tablespoons wholemeal (wholewheat) flour

3 tablespoons polenta (cornmeal)

about 2 cups (500 mL/16 fl oz) canola oil for frying

Serves 4–6

163

Simplicity itself, this tasty dish is lovely served with Quick Cashew Rice (page 108).

Ingredients

1 cup (20 g/¾ oz) dried Chinese (shiitake) mushrooms

1 cup (250 mL/ 8 fl oz) boiling water

1–2 tablespoons soy sauce

3 teaspoons sesame oil

pepper

500 g (1 lb) firm tofu, drained and cut into cubes or strips

6 spring onions (scallions), sliced, green tops included

2–3 garlic cloves, crushed (pressed)

1 red capsicum (sweet pepper), cut into strips

250 g (8 oz) green beans, sliced

2 teaspoons arrowroot

1 tablespoon mirin *or* dry sherry *or* apple juice

Serves 6

Method

Place the mushrooms in a heatproof bowl and pour over the water. Set the mushrooms aside to soak for 20 minutes.

Meanwhile, combine the soy sauce, 1 teaspoon of the oil and pepper and brush over the tofu slices.

Grill (broil) under a medium-high heat for 5 minutes each side. Set aside.

Heat the remaining oil in a wok and stir-fry the spring onion, garlic, capsicum and beans for 5 minutes.

Drain the mushrooms, retaining the soaking water.

Using kitchen scissors, snip the stalks from the mushrooms, then slice the mushroom tops and add them to the vegetables in the wok.

Place the arrowroot in a small bowl and blend to a smooth paste with a little of the mushroom soaking water.

Add the remaining mushroom water and stir into the vegetables.

Cook, stirring for 1 minute, then add the tofu and cook gently for 5 minutes.

Stir in the mirin (or sherry or apple juice) and serve.

Flavoursome Dried Mushrooms

Dried Chinese mushrooms are also known as shiitake mushrooms. They are great to have tucked away in the pantry because they keep almost indefinitely. Commonly used in Asian cooking, dried shiitake must be reconstituted by soaking for 20–30 minutes before use. The stalks, which are very tough, are usually removed after the soaking process. I find the easiest way to do this is to snip them off with a pair of kitchen scissors. Shiitake mushrooms have a wonderful chewy texture and a superb full-bodied flavour; in fact, they are so flavoursome that a tasty vegetable stock can even be made from the water they have been soaked in. They are available from Asian grocery stores and health food stores.

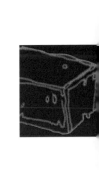

Tempeh

Tempeh is a firm cake of partially cooked fermented soy beans, entwined by a soft downy mould culture similar to the 'crust' on fresh ripened cheeses such as Camembert and Brie. Tempeh's firm texture makes it easy to handle. It can be cut into slices, strips or cubes and is best quickly fried in a little oil. I rarely use frying as a cooking method, but I must admit with tempeh, this method really brings out the flavour and produces a scrumptious golden-brown crust on the outside. So enjoy these Golden Tempeh Croutons (opposite) conscience-free by serving them as part of a low-fat meal with soup, stir-fried vegetables and salad. Also see 'Healthy Tips for Deep-frying', on page 161. Tempeh can also be marinated and oven-baked until golden-brown as for Soy-doused Tofu Croutons (page 159) if you prefer. Tempeh is available from Asian grocery stores and health food stores.

These crunchy little golden morsels are perfect for adding to stir-fries just before serving, or offering as a little nibble with a tasty dipping sauce. Also great for sprinkling over thick soups or scattered though salads instead of the usual croutons made from bread.

Method

Cut the tempeh into 1-cm (½-in) cubes.

Heat the oil in a frying pan (skillet) until it bubbles up immediately when a cube of tempeh is added.

Add the tempeh gradually and cook until it becomes golden-brown.

Remove straightaway from the oil, using a slotted spoon, and drain thoroughly on brown paper or absorbent kitchen towels.

Serve at once or store in a covered container in the refrigerator for 2–3 days or freeze.

Ingredients

375 g (13 oz) tempeh

peanut (groundnut) oil for frying

Serves 4

Soy Drink

A wide variety of plain and flavoured soy drinks are available these days. You can even buy reduced-fat varieties which have been produced in response to the low-fat 'bent' of today's consumer. Use it in place of cow's milk in all recipes. The bonus of including soy drinks in your cooking is that the fats they contain are largely polyunsaturated, and are more beneficial for good health than the saturated fats contained in full-fat dairy products.

Delicious

Dairy Foods

Not only can dairy foods be whipped up into quick meals, but they also provide vital nutrients, variety and interest in our day-to-day meals. Nowadays there is an amazing variety of dairy foods readily available to us.

Even sour cream is available in a reduced-fat variety which contains about half the fat of regular sour cream without losing its delightful creamy texture. Yoghurt, too, has come a long way in the last few years. Once upon a time, yoghurt was something that health nuts endured. Now it is a food savoured by many of us who love dolloping it on top of fresh fruit and muesli for breakfast, and on to piping hot soups, baked jacket potatoes and hot and spicy bean dishes for special snacks and light meals.

Milk

Milk can be incorporated into many dishes from super smoothies and thick or elegant soups to lovely sauces. And low-fat varieties can be used in most recipes without being noticed. Many people rely on milk for their daily quota of calcium, phosphorous, vitamins A and D and riboflavin (a vitamin of the B complex). So here are some quick and tasty ways to enjoy these nutrients.

The tangy sweetness of fresh strawberries offsets the creamy texture of the blended banana in this delicious recipe. And the pink hue imparted by the strawberries makes it even more appetising.

Method

Place all the ingredients in a blender or food processor and mix for 30 seconds or so, making sure all the fruit has been blended until it is velvety smooth.

Enjoy at once.

Ingredients

1 ripe banana, peeled and cut into chunks

2 ice cubes

2 cups (500 mL/ 16 fl oz) low-fat milk

2 tablespoons yoghurt (optional)

a few fresh strawberries, washed and hulled

Serves 2

Note for Doubling Fruit Flavour

Use frozen fruit juice or frozen berries instead of ice cubes to add flavour as well as the big chill to your next smoothie. Start preparing now by pouring some fruit juice in an ice-cube tray to freeze. Or try a double banana flavoured smoothie, by freezing some peeled chunks of banana so they will be ready to pop into your next smoothie instead of ice cubes.

Super Special Smoothies

These are so good that you can make a satisfying breakfast or light meal from them. All you have to do is add a small handful of nuts to the blender. And what better way to end a summer meal than with a super special smoothie served in a parfait glass with sliced fresh fruit adorning the side of the glass, Carmen Miranda style? The main tip to remember with fresh fruit smoothies is that they are best consumed straightaway when the flavour is fresh and 'alive'.

Apricots with their full sweet flavour make great smoothies, even in the cooler months when fresh apricots are not available locally. In summer though, do try using fresh sun-ripened fruit to give that unmistakable 'oomph' to this delicious drink.

Method

Ingredients

½ cup (125 mL/ 4 fl oz) apricot nectar

½ cup (125 mL/ 4 fl oz) plain yoghurt

1 cup (250 mL/ 8 fl oz) low-fat milk

2–3 ice cubes

6 fresh or canned (tinned) apricot halves, drained

cinnamon

Serves 2

Using a blender or food processor, blend all the ingredients except the cinnamon, until the mixture becomes velvety smooth.

Serve with a light dusting of cinnamon.

Yoghurt

It seems yoghurt is fast becoming one of the most popular dairy foods around. It is widely available from supermarkets in all sizes of containers from snack to economy-size tubs to keep a whole family going for days. You can buy non-fat, reduced-fat, full-cream or fruit-packed varieties, and some even come packaged with fruit sauces, muesli and their own spoon. Not bad for a food that was dismissed as a fad food some years back! Enjoy incorporating yoghurt into delicious dips, dressings, sauces, breakfasts and desserts. I have a feeling it's here to stay, and to that, all I have to say is — hooray!

Roasted red capsicum (sweet pepper) come up trumps here with its rich sweet flavour and brilliant hue shining through in this quick dip. Serve with fresh, lightly steamed vegetables and some fresh crusty bread. By the way, this dip makes a great sandwich spread too.

Ingredients

2 red capsicums (sweet peppers), roasted and peeled (page 16) and additional finely shredded red capsicum for garnishing

250 g (8 oz) light cream cheese or soft tofu

2 garlic cloves, crushed (pressed)

pepper

few drops Tabasco Sauce

cracked black pepper for garnishing

Makes about 1½ cups (375 mL/ 12 fl oz)

Method

Using a food processor, blend the capsicum, cream cheese (or tofu) and garlic until smooth.

Season to taste with the pepper and Tabasco Sauce, then serve topped with the finely shredded capsicum and dusted with pepper.

Cucumber dip, or raita, as it is sometimes called, is often served with hot spicy dishes because of its cooling qualities. Perhaps that is where the saying 'cool as a cucumber' comes from! This dip is also delicious served with warmed pita bread and fresh, blanched or roasted vegetables, or spooned over Baked Jacket Potatoes (page 59), right next to a generous spoonful of Chilli Beans (page 151).

Method

Cut the cucumber in half lengthways and scoop out the pips, using a metal teaspoon.

Dice the flesh finely.

Place the cucumber in a bowl, combine with the yoghurt, cream cheese, garlic, Tabasco Sauce, lemon juice, chives (or spring onion) and pepper, and dust with the paprika.

Ingredients

1 medium-sized cucumber, peeled

1 cup (250 mL/ 8 fl oz) plain yoghurt

125 g (4 oz) light cream cheese

3 garlic cloves, crushed (pressed)

few drops Tabasco Sauce

juice of ½ lemon, about 2 tablespoons

3 tablespoons finely sliced chives or spring onions (scallions), green tops included

pepper

ground sweet paprika

Makes about 1½ cups (375 mL/ 12 fl oz)

Cheese

Be adventurous — visit your local fresh food market or delicatessen and look out for one or two varieties of cheese you have never tried before. Ask the proprietor of the shop how to use them and enjoy incorporating them into your meals even if you just add one or two wedges on a platter for friends and family to taste. With the enormous range of exciting cheeses available now, I send a heartfelt thanks to the people who make up our multicultural society. Now 'cherries' refer to more than the delectable ruby red fruit variety, for baby unripened mozzarella cheeses are usually referred to as bocconcini cherries. These are delightful little morsels of creamy white cheese which lend themselves beautifully to antipasto platters, salads, sandwiches and special pizzas. There are wonderful low-fat cheeses readily available at supermarkets and delicatessens such as ricotta cheese and quark (rather like a smooth cottage cheese) which are great for whipping up into a frenzy of dips or for serving with roasted vegetables. And watch out for a real all-time favourite ingredient for dips and cheesecakes — cream cheese. Like many dairy foods, it is also available in reduced-fat varieties and is absolutely luscious blended with a little honey and finely grated lemon rind (see Lemon Cream Cheese on page 184).

Simple yet delectable, this salad is surprisingly satisfying when served with roasted vegetables and plenty of bread. The pesto-tinted bocconcini surrounded by the rich red of the tomatoes looks fabulous served amidst crisp fresh greens. My first choice of greens for this salad would be rocket (arugula) leaves because of the peppery edge to their flavour. Next, I would go for the tender inner leaves of curly endive (frisée) with their bitter sweet taste, or young radicchio with its crimson-streaked leaves and distinctive bitter edge. When tiny yellow tomatoes are in season, add several as a golden highlight to this pretty salad.

Method

Combine the Pesto Sauce and the lemon juice in a medium-sized bowl.

Add the bocconcini cherries and toss through the pesto mixture so that they become evenly coated with it.

Arrange the greens on 1 large or 4 individual serving plates and pile a little mound of bocconcini in the middle.

Sprinkle with the parsley, and arrange the tomatoes amongst the leaves.

Dust all with pepper, pop the lemon wedges on the side and garnish with basil leaves.

Ingredients

2 tablespoons
Pesto Sauce
(page 92)

juice of
1 lemon, about
4 tablespoons, and
4 lemon wedges for
serving

325 g (12 oz)
bocconcini cherries,
drained well and
cut in half

3 cups green leafy
vegetables, such as
rocket (arugula) or
curly endive (frisée)

¼ cup chopped
Italian (flat-leaf)
parsley

1 punnet (carton)
cherry tomatoes

cracked black
pepper

a few fresh basil
leaves for
garnishing

Serves 4

Bocconcini Cheese

A soft fresh cheese, bocconcini has a firm curd and slices well. It is relatively low in fat and is delightful used in salads, savouries, pizza toppings and casseroles and braises.

Pesto *Cream*

Snazzy but simple, this dish can be used as a dip, to fill cannelloni shells or sandwiches or as a light yet flavour-packed layer in your next lasagne.

Method

Ingredients

½ cup (60 g/2 oz) pine nuts, roasted

½ bunch basil, chopped

½ cup chopped parsley

250 g (8 oz) ricotta cheese, drained

3 garlic cloves, crushed (pressed)

cracked black pepper

Makes about 1½ cups (375 mL/12 fl oz)

Using a food processor, process the pine nuts to a meal.

Add the basil and parsley and process further.

Then, with a wooden spoon, combine the ricotta with the garlic and the pepper, and beat in the pine nut mixture.

This is a scrumptious recipe which can be whipped up in a matter of minutes. Try serving it with fresh carrot and celery sticks, with a bowl of corn chips nearby. It also doubles as a wonderful sandwich filling.

Method

Place all the ingredients except for the additional peanuts in a food processor and blend until smooth.

Ingredients

250 g (8 oz) ricotta cheese, drained

½ cup (75 g/ 2½ oz) roasted peanuts (groundnuts) and additional roasted peanuts for garnishing

1–2 garlic cloves, crushed (pressed)

1 tablespoon tahini

2 tablespoons soy sauce

few drops of Tabasco Sauce (optional)

pepper

Makes about 1½ cups (375 mL/ 12 fl oz)

Ricotta Cheese

Ricotta is a relatively low-fat cheese with a soft texture and a slightly sweet, bland flavour. It can be used in a myriad of dishes such as dips, dressings, terrines, pasta, desserts and cheesecakes. Being a fresh cheese, it should only be purchased in an amount that you are likely to use well within the week. You can buy firm ricotta cheese, suitable for slicing and baking, and smooth ricotta which is ideal for dips, spreads, desserts and cheesecakes.

Serve with a simple tasty sauce such as Scarlet Sauce (page 17) and topped with a little extra Parmesan. Or, for something different, try adding these little dumplings to a pot of hot soup such as a herbed tomato soup, at the end of the cooking time.

Method

Ingredients

250 g (8 oz) ricotta cheese, drained

½ cup finely sliced chives

1 egg, beaten

3 tablespoons grated Parmesan cheese

¼ teaspoon pepper

½–¾ cup (2–3 oz) unbleached white flour

Serves 4

Begin by boiling 3 litres (3 quarts/ 4¾ imp pints) water (or stock) (see page 18).

Meanwhile, combine the ricotta, chives, egg, Parmesan and pepper well.

Mix in enough flour to form a soft dough (batter).

Form the dough into 4 pieces and roll each piece into a long roll about 1½ cm (½ in) thick.

Using a sharp knife, cut the rolls of dough into 1½-cm (¾-in) pieces to form gnocchi.

When the water (or stock) is boiling, add the gnocchi and cook until they all rise to the surface, about 5 minutes.

Using a large slotted spoon, remove the gnocchi as soon as they are cooked.

This is ideally a summer dish because fresh basil and sun-ripened tomatoes are at their best then. The wonderful flavour and fragrance of the fresh basil leaves offsets the salty flavour of haloumi beautifully. Make sure you have a supply of fresh crusty bread on hand and a crisp green salad. I love serving a simple salad of peppery rocket (arugula) leaves with haloumi, or you could try young radicchio leaves if, as I do, you appreciate its distinctive bitter edge.

Method

Place the haloumi cheese in a medium-sized bowl and cover it with cold water. Allow to stand for 1 hour if possible, so that much of the salt is released.

Drain the haloumi and pat dry with a clean tea towel.

Cut it into ½-cm (¼-in) slices.

Using a pastry brush to ensure that the bottom of the pan is evenly coated, brush a frying pan (skillet) with the oil.

When the pan is hot, add the haloumi slices and cook for 2–3 minutes on each side or until the cheese becomes golden-brown.

Arrange on a large platter or individual plates with the tomato slices.

Dust with the pepper, scatter the basil leaves over and serve with the lemon wedges.

Ingredients

500 g (1 lb) haloumi cheese

1 tablespoon olive oil

4 good-sized sun-ripened tomatoes, cut into thick crossways slices

cracked black pepper

16–20 good-sized fresh basil leaves

4–6 lemon wedges

Serves 4–6

Haloumi Cheese

A stretchy curd cheese, haloumi is matured and stored in brine like feta. It has a firm compact texture and slices well, but usually has a very salty flavour. This can be rectified by soaking it in milk or water for an hour or two. Then drain the cheese well and pat it dry with paper towels or a clean tea towel before using. Use it sliced or diced and added to salads, soups and braises, or fry it Greek-style until golden-brown in a little olive oil.

Serve as an appetiser or finger food, or, for a snack or light meal, serve with wedges of ripe tomato and some fresh crusty bread.

Method

Ingredients

250 g (8 oz) feta cheese, drained

¼ teaspoon cracked black pepper

1 cup chopped parsley

16 large basil leaves

16 toothpicks (cocktail sticks)

Makes 16 parcels

Cut the feta into 16 cubes about 2 cm x 3 cm (¾ in x 1 in).

Sprinkle with the pepper.

Place the parsley on a plate and roll the feta cubes in the parsley to coat them.

Wrap each cube of feta in a basil leaf and secure with a toothpick.

Have You Tried Feta Cheese?

Feta is a white or pale cream Greek-style cheese generally made from goat's or sheep's milk but can also be made from cow's milk. It is matured and stored in a brine solution, its sharp salty flavour making it a wonderful companion for spinach and tomato dishes.

These are delightful served with Scarlet Sauce (page 17) or Quick Tomato Chutney (page 24) for dipping.

Method

Preheat the oven to 200°C/400°F.

Cut the cheese into 16 pieces about 2 cm x 3 cm (¾ in x 1 in) and place in a mixing bowl.

Combine 2 teaspoons of the oil with the garlic and pepper.

Then, using your hands, carefully toss the cheese in the mixture and coat it well.

Cut the filo sheets in half crossways, stack one on top of the other and position the sheets with the shortest sides opposite you.

Place each cube of feta on the end of the sheet closest to you and fold the two long sides over the feta.

Roll the feta up inside the filo to form small parcels.

Place the parcels on a baking tray (sheet) that has been brushed with a little oil.

Brush the parcels lightly with oil and sprinkle with the poppy seeds.

Bake in a hot oven for 15 minutes or until the parcels become golden-brown.

Ingredients

250 g/8 oz feta cheese, drained

8 sheets filo (phyllo) pastry

3 teaspoons olive oil

2 garlic cloves, crushed (pressed)

¼ teaspoon cracked black pepper

1–2 tablespoons poppy seeds

Makes 16 parcels

Squeezed through a large piping bag, Lemon Cream Cheese transforms even the simplest of foods into a tantalising treat. It's a wonder that I haven't piped it all over our cats while they sleep — I seem to have covered anything else that has stood still long enough! Seriously though, I have found so many uses for this creamy delight — it is best piped on to edible treats like freshly made hot cakes, scones and muffins, or used to stuff fresh fruit such as large strawberries and dates, or halved apricots, peaches and plums. It makes a great dip too, for wedges of melon or luscious fingers of firm-fleshed ripe pineapple. And so on and so on ...

Method

Ingredients

500 g (1 lb) cream cheese

3 teaspoons Orange Blossom Honey (page 69)

1 teaspoon finely grated lemon rind

Makes about 2 cups (500 mL/16 fl oz)

First, soften the cream cheese by placing it in a microwave-proof bowl and heat on medium-low for 1 minute.

Alternatively, place the cream cheese in a heatproof bowl and stand it in the sink with 2–3 cm (about 1 in) of hot water.

Using a wooden spoon, beat in the honey, then the lemon rind.

Place the mixture in an attractive serving bowl if using it for dipping.

If you wish to run amok piping it on all and sundry as I do, place the mixture in a large piping bag and pipe away to your heart's content.

Cream Cheese

Smooth, rich and mildly flavoured, cream cheese is excellent for making dips, dessert and cake toppings and cheesecakes. Try to find cream cheese with a reduced fat content, like Light Philadelphia or Neufchatel, because full-fat cream cheese contains at least 33% fat.

Index